SOCRATES

SOCRATES.

A Translation

OF THE

APOLOGY, CRITO, AND PARTS OF THE PHAEDO

OF

PLATO.

GYAN

Published by

Gyan Publishing House
5, Ansari Road
Daryaganj, New Delhi-110002
Phone: 011-47034999, 9811692060
E-mail: books@gyanbooks.com

Distribution Network
gyanbooks.com
India, USA, Canada, UK, Australia

ISBN: 978-81-212-8408-0 (HB)
First Published, 1886

2nd Impression 2024

Printed at: Gyan Press, Delhi.

SOCRATES
Author: PLATO

SOCRATES.

SOCRATES.

A Translation

OF THE

APOLOGY, CRITO, AND PARTS OF THE PHAEDO

OF

PLATO.

SIXTH EDITION.

NEW YORK:
CHARLES SCRIBNER'S SONS,
1886.

INTRODUCTION.

I HAVE advised the translator to publish these versions of Plato, in the belief that they will be welcomed by many to whom both Plato and Socrates have hitherto been merely venerated names, especially by those whose interest in knowing what Plato and Socrates really taught has been doubly checked, by ignorance of Greek, and by the formidable aspect of Plato's Complete Works even in an English translation. This volume offers a new translation of the parts of Plato which are most essential to an understanding of the personal character and the moral position of Socrates, and includes a famous specimen of Plato's own speculations on one of the grandest subjects. The translator has avoided successfully, as it seems to me, the harshness of a strictly literal version on the one side, and the inexactness of a mere paraphrase on the other: the aim has been to make the translation readable, and still to retain, as far as possible, whatever is characteristic of the original, even its occasional prolixity. It must be remembered that no translation of an ancient author — not even Browning's verbal "transcript" of the Agamemnon — can be both perfectly exact and perfectly intelligible; and it is not long since it was true of Plato, as it still remains true of Aristotle, that there was no English translation by which any one could understand his most important works without the aid of the Greek.

The Apology, giving Plato's report of the memorable Defence which he had heard from his master's lips in the Athenian court, shows the eccentric but sturdy independence of Socrates, the inflexible resolution with which he executed what he believed to be a divine command, and the calm fearlessness with which he announced to the court that he should obey God rather than man, and that no human power should compel him to desert his post. It also gives an amusing account of the manner in which Socrates went about his work of exposing ignorance and convicting imposture. The Crito gives us an opposite, but no less striking, view of the character of Socrates, showing the real respect for the laws and institutions of his country which he felt under all his defiant independence. It contains the eloquent argument in which he scornfully refuses to insult the authority of the state, under the protection of which he had lived, by escaping through flight from the execution of even an unjust sentence, especially when all that could be gained by such an ignominious act would be a short prolongation of an almost finished life. These two discourses thus exhibit Socrates as equally stubborn in upholding the supremacy of duty above all human power, and in recognizing the supremacy of law above all personal considerations and even above life itself; he is, moreover, in contrast to many later martyrs, both willing and determined to die in defence of either of these positions. In the Phaedo we have the affecting narrative of the closing scene in the life of Socrates, with the conversation on the soul and immortality which Plato represents him as holding with his friends during the few last hours before he drank the hemlock. Of this dialogue the narrative part is given in full, while many of the discussions are judiciously abridged by omitting large portions of the argument which appeared to the translator to have lost their interest for the present age or to be too abstruse for a work like the present. Abstracts of the argument of the omitted passages (which amount to a little more than half of the Phaedo) are given in the proper places.

When we pass from the Apology, and even the narrative parts of the Phaedo, to the philosophical discussions of the latter, we notice a great change in the more dogmatic tone assumed by Socrates. We have, in fact, here suddenly passed from the Socratic to the Platonic Socrates. Plato was in the habit of using his master in his dialogues as a mouth-piece for the expression of his own speculations; and he thus makes him utter many doctrines which the real Socrates would hardly have understood, and many which that rigid questioner would have subjected to a merciless cross-examination. Among these is Plato's doctrine of independent ideal forms, which we know, from Aristotle, was never developed by Socrates himself, although he laid its foundation by teaching the importance of general conceptions as the basis of all sound philosophy. Yet we find this doctrine expounded in great detail by Socrates in the Phaedo, and made the basis of an elaborate argument for the immortality of the soul. We must remember that the Socrates of these discourses is in great measure Plato himself, expounding—under his master's name and with much of his master's manner—doctrines of his own, which he had developed under the inspiration of the teachings of Socrates, or which he believed Socrates would have approved if he could have lived to appreciate them. Thus the doctrine of immortality appears in the Phaedo, the Phaedrus, and the Republic essentially enlarged and modified by the Platonic doctrines of ideas and of reminiscence, and by including the preëxistence of the soul, so as to be far more Platonic than Socratic. The opinion of the real Socrates on these subjects may be inferred from his remark in the Apology, that, if there is any one point on which he would claim to be wiser than other men, it is this, that having no better knowledge than others of the world to come, he is likewise convinced that he has none. The same is true of all the dogmatic discourses on speculative subjects which are ascribed to Socrates by Plato. Still we must remember that it is through Plato that his master is best known; and it is the Platonic Socrates quite as much as the real Socrates who has passed into history. Even Aristotle often quotes Plato's doctrines under the name of Socrates.

When we turn to the Apology, we find the genuine Socrates, the same plain, unpretending inquirer whose portrait has been drawn from another point of view by Xenophon in his Memorabilia. In the Apology, too, we hear the hum of the real gadfly (as Socrates called himself) which buzzed about the ears of the venerable Demos of Athens and stung that "testy old man" to madness until he could bear the infliction no longer. Socrates never professed to be a teacher in the ordinary sense of that word; he called himself an examiner. He felt that the great enemy of truth in Athens was not ignorance, pure and simple, — this he could leave to schoolmasters to enlighten, — but ignorance puffed up with the conceit of knowledge. This was the fatal disease with which Socrates spent the best strength of his life in struggling,

It met him at every turn, and he encountered it with his searching questions. The politicians, he reports, were easy victims of his cross-examination. He next tried the tragedians, as well as the dithyrambic and other poets, and found that they wrote "by nature and inspiration," not by knowledge. We should be glad to know whether he extended his missionary visits to Sophocles, Euripides, and Aristophanes, and how they received him if he did. As to Aristophanes, we may perhaps gather from the last scene of Plato's Symposium — where we find Socrates and Aristophanes left alone with the host at the supper-table "after cock-crowing," engaged in an animated discussion, over their wine, of the relation of comedy to tragedy — that the comedian and the philosopher were not on bad terms socially. Still the result of his tormenting examinations was a general enmity against Socrates among the public men and the poets of Athens. When he came to the mechanics, he found some improvement, inasmuch as these proved to be excellently taught in their own trades; but this very knowledge had filled them with a delusion that they knew all about the greatest subjects also, of which they really knew nothing. Socrates here saw one of the inevitable results of a general diffusion of intelligence in a free community. He would not have found the same trouble among the mechanics of Thebes, nor should we find it among those of Naples. But where the people are stimulated to think at all, they will think on the highest subjects; and the greatest service that could be rendered, not merely to them, but to the states for which they legislate, would be just that which Socrates undertook for the people of Athens, to show them the distinction between irrational opinion and true knowledge, and to induce them to test their opinions by ex amination and discussion. Whether a missionary who should undertake this work in a modern city, in the manner of "a father or an elder brother," would fare better than Socrates did in ancient Athens, may well be doubted. But there can be no doubt that more of the Socratic spirit of inquiry, and more of the Socrati faith in virtue, are the imperative needs of every demo cratic state.

W. W. GOODWIN.

HARVARD UNIVERSITY, *November*, 1878.

PREFACE.

In presenting to the reader these translations, which describe the closing scenes in the life of Socrates, it may not be out of place to give, as far as possible in the words of his contemporaries, a slight sketch of the sage himself and his surroundings.

Socrates was born in 469 B. C. The son of Sophroniscus, a poor sculptor of little repute, he was compelled to follow his father's profession for a livelihood; and it is said to have been only through the generosity of his friend Crito that he was enabled, at about the age of thirty, to devote himself to philosophy. According to some writers, however, he was already at this time proficient in both literature and gymnastics, which constituted the ordinary education of the day, and, moreover, had studied under the most celebrated teachers of that period. Yet his own words would lead us to infer that he had received but little special philosophic training; for he speaks of having attended merely the single-drachma course of Prodicus the grammarian, because the fifty-drachma lectures, which "to hear only"—we quote the teacher's own words—"was to become thoroughly educated on their subject-matter," were beyond his means![1] We may well doubt, however, whether the wishes of this

[1] Plat. Cratylus, 384 B.

"self-taught philosopher," for so Socrates speaks of himself, would have impelled him to follow any of the so-called guides of the day, for he seems early to have reached the conclusion that, however gladly he might sit at the feet of the man who could show him where to find that "cause" or "power which binds and holds all together," he should "never be able to learn this from any one."[1]

In the Phaedo we shall find his own account of his researches and disappointed hopes, and of his final conviction that only by working from within outwards, and not, as had hitherto been attempted, by means of investigations in the outer world, can truth be reached; while in the Apology he describes the manner in which he fulfilled his divinely appointed mission, and enforced upon other men the result of his own experience, that "a life without self-examination is not worth living,"[2] and that "he is wisest who, like Socrates, has come to know that he in truth is worth nothing as regards wisdom."[3]

The message of the Delphic oracle, in obedience to which this life-long task was assumed, came to him in middle age, and was perhaps, in substance, little else than the summing up of the conclusions at which he had himself arrived. Solely, indeed, to the strength of these, his own unaided convictions, might we be tempted to ascribe the impulse which led him on, for we cannot but feel the character of the man and of his teaching to be inconsistent with literal obedience to such supernatural agencies as this of Delphi. But we must remember that Socrates was a man of his time, and saw no reason for doubting oracles, dreams, and omens, even while acknowledging the one great beneficent Power which decrees

[1] Plat. Phaedo, 99 C. [2] Apology, 38 A. [3] Apology, 23 B.

that "no evil can befall a good man, whether he be alive or dead."[1] We cannot doubt, therefore, that coming as the message did from the shrine holiest of all in the eyes of the ancient world, over whose portal was inscribed that motto which formed the rule of his own life, "Know thyself," he must have felt that he was singled out by God to accomplish a divine purpose. From this time he devoted himself with redoubled zeal to that which heretofore had been a self-imposed task, but which now appeared in the light of a message entrusted to him from on high. For this object all other interests and claims were set aside. "Neglectful," he says, "of what most men prize, money-making, family interests, military command, public speaking, and all offices of the state,[2] . . . . I have never had the leisure to do anything worth speaking of, either in the state or for my own household, so that I am in very great poverty by reason of my service to the God."[3]

It seemed but fitting that so marked an individuality as that of Socrates should be invested with a bodily frame equally singular and striking. We frequently meet with playful allusions to that peculiar physiognomy which was likened by himself and his friends to "the masks of the Sileni to be seen in the workshops of the statuaries." The likeness to the Satyr Marsyas, in particular, was, they declared, yet heightened by the musical skill of each; although in this respect Socrates was held the superior of the two, for while Marsyas "charmed men by means of instruments, Socrates did the same by use of words alone."

This strange figure, unshod, and always clad in the same poor cloak, which served for all seasons of the year,

[1] Apology, 41 D. [2] Apology, 36 B. [3] Apology, 23 B.

must have been familiar to every Athenian; for, as Xen ophon tells us, "he was always before men's sight. Early in the morning he went to the public walks and gymnasia; when the market was full, he was to be seen there; and all the rest of the day he always went wherever he could meet most people."[1] Under plea of seeking information, he would enter the workshops of the mechanics and sculptors, or converse, whenever opportunity offered, with poet, philosopher, politician, and citizen, always exciting in his hearer the same wonder at his intimate knowledge of each one's specialty. Even to the convivial gatherings of the wealthy Athenians he did not neglect a summons, and there too his power of adaptation made him an ever-welcome guest.

The thick-set, muscular frame of Socrates, his ungainly movements and awkward gait, — his whole appearance, indeed, — bespoke the great physical strength so often brought into requisition to withstand tests of the severest kind. How well he succeeded in subduing the claims of the body may be gathered from an incident which occurred when he was under arms in the camp at Potidaea. It was one day observed that he had been standing in the same position from dawn till noontide, apparently lost in thought over some problem which he was seeking to solve. "Then," as Alcibiades relates in the Symposium, "people began to notice him, and to relate to one another with wonder that Socrates had been stand ing there, pondering, ever since daybreak. At last evening came, and some of the Ionians, after they had supped, brought out their mats and slept in the open air (for it was summer), partly to enjoy the cool, and partly to watch Socrates and see whether he would really remain

[1] Xen. Mem. i. 1, 10.

all night. Well, there he stood until the day broke and the sun had risen, and then, after he had offered a prayer to the sun-god, he went away."[1]

On the several occasions on which he bore arms for his country, the wonder of his fellow-soldiers was constantly awakened by the fortitude he displayed. In the expedition to Potidaea, we are told, "he exceeded by far all others in power of sustaining hunger," although, it is slyly remarked, "he enjoyed a feast more than any of us." Of his indifference to cold we learn that "once, in particular, when there was such a terrible frost that we hardly dared go out at all, or if we were obliged to go, we went wrapped up in the most wonderful manner, our feet not only shod, but swathed in felt and sheepskins, he sallied forth in the same cloak which he was in the habit of wearing every day, and walked upon the ice with bare feet far more easily than did the others in their shoes; insomuch that the soldiers eyed him suspiciously, thinking that he was setting himself up above them." And in proof of his courage in battle, Alcibiades relates: "In one engagement, it was no other than Socrates who saved my life; for when I was wounded he would not leave me, and not only rescued me, but my arms also. I urged the generals on that occasion to give him the prize of valour which they had awarded to me, but he was yet more eager than they that I and not he should receive it. And again, when the army was fleeing from Delium, it was a sight indeed to behold Socrates. I happened to meet him when he was carrying his heavy arms, while I was on horseback. The army was all disbanded, and he and

[1] Plat. Sympos. 220. For this and the following selections from the Symposium, the translator is indebted to the kindness of Professor Goodwin.

Laches were retreating together; and I observed how far superior he was to Laches in presence of mind, for he appeared then, just as you, Aristophanes, have described him, stalking about there, as he does here to-day, his head erect and rolling his eyes and calmly scrutinizing friend and foe. It was plain to see, even from distance, that if any one were to lay hands upon this man he would stoutly defend himself. And on this very account he and his companion got off safely; for in war such persons are seldom touched; it is they who flee headlong who are pursued."[1] And Laches himself is made to bear this testimony to the valour and example of Socrates: "In the flight from Delium he was my companion, and I can tell you that, if others had been like him, our country would have maintained its honour, and not had to mourn such a defeat."[2]

To realize the revolution created by Socrates both in the intellectual and in the moral sphere, it would be necessary to trace the previous history of philosophic thought, a task beyond the compass of this sketch. Suffice it to say, that, while diametrically opposed to the Physicists, whose attempt to "reason upon the nature of all things and to find out how that which the Sophists call *the world* was created, and by what necessity everything in the heavens takes place,"[3] he characterizes as a "mad" one, he equally disavowed connection with the various schools of teachers — classed together under the common name of Sophists — which had lately arisen to meet the changed requirements of the day. Positive knowledge, indeed, Socrates did not profess to impart, since for this, in common with his followers, he avowed himself to be but a

[1] Plat. Sympos. 220, 221.
[2] Plat. Laches, 181.
[3] Xen. Mem. i. 1, 11.

fellow-seeker. He aimed rather at furnishing a method by which men should be enabled to clear away the superstructure of false knowledge which had been allowed to crowd out their inborn conceptions of goodness and truth, and to apply these principles to questions of practical morality. "Calling down," says Cicero, "Philosophy from the heavens, he placed her in cities, introduced her into private families, and compelled her to inquire concerning human life, morals, and the good and evil of every notion."[1] "He was always," Xenophon tells us, "discoursing upon human duties, examining what was pious or impious, good or bad, just or unjust, foolish or wise, brave or cowardly; and he considered that the men who had knowledge upon these subjects were good and noble, while they who had not this knowledge might rightly, in his opinion, be called slaves."[2]

The exact religious belief of Socrates it is impossible to define; yet we cannot but feel certain that he believed in one Supreme Being, whose voice he undoubtedly recognized in the message of the Delphic oracle. He frequently, however, adopts the language of the day, possibly for the sake of reaching the understanding of all, and uses the name of Deity both with the definite article and in the plural number. But if, as we may well believe, he held the common deities to be attributes of or emanations from the one God, he is not open to the charge of using an inconsistent or misleading mode of speech, for in yielding them reverence he was but paying the homage due to all members or parts of the great Whole. Oracles and prophecies he seems to have regarded in the light of intermediary agencies, through which messages were conveyed from heaven to earth.

[1] Cic. Tusc. Disp. v. 4, 10. [2] Xen. Mem. i. 1, 16.

"For God," as he was taught to believe by the wise Diotima, "has no direct communication with man."[1]

About his divine voice, familiar spirit, or daemon, as it has been severally called by his biographers, conjecture has been endlessly busy, nor does Socrates himself help us to form any decided opinion as to its nature. Regarding it however, as he did, in the light of a special manifestation of the divine will, "a thing rarely if ever before vouchsafed to any man,"[2] we cannot be surprised that with his reverent nature he should have yielded to it the most implicit obedience. "If he thought," says Xenophon, "that he had received any intimation from the Gods, he would have been less easily persuaded to act against it than he could have been persuaded to take as a guide a blind man and one ignorant of the road in preference to one who both saw and knew the way."[3]

In many sentences put into the mouth of Socrates, as well as in others where Plato, although not directly quoting his master, was yet probably inspired by him, we meet with ideas which, far removed from those common to the Greek world, approach even the Christian standard. His warning that if we would become the friend of God who is perfect, we must make ourselves like unto him, and become even as he is,[4] reminds us of another exhortation to be "perfect, even as your Father which is in heaven is perfect." His reverent compliance with many religious usages, which were consecrated by age and custom, did not prevent him from denouncing the abuses and prejudices connected with sacrificial worship, or protesting against those who believed that the Gods were to be propitiated with sacrifice.[5] The Ho-

1 Plat. Sympos. 203 A
2 Ib. Rep. 496 C.
3 Xen. Mem. i. 3, 4.
4 Laws, 716; see also Rep. 381.
5 Plat. Laws, 909.

meric assertion that the Gods are careless and passively allow evil to have its way, he strongly denounces;[1] and holds as nothing short of impious the belief that God, being good himself, can be "the cause of evil to any man."[2] While assuring us of a loving providence which suffers men to be corrected only that they may become better, he yet brings home to us this solemn warning: "O youth or young man, who thinkest thyself to be unheeded by the Gods, art thou even so small as to sink into the depths of the earth, or so high as to fly up to heaven, thou shalt still pay the fitting penalty which they will exact."[3] To us who are living in the full light of Christianity and enjoying the fruits of a purer teaching than the ancient world ever knew, the effect produced upon the minds of his hearers by the lessons of religion and morality enforced by Socrates may well seem incomprehensible. But although many of his teachings appear to us to-day mere truisms, if we bear in mind their entire opposition to current opinion, and the absolutely different standard which they inculcated, we may realize that what to the purest and most earnest minds came as a message of truth and hope, appeared to the mass of men a startling and ill-judged interference with established doctrines.

For the unpopularity, then, of Socrates we have not far to seek. It must indeed be considered a proof of the extreme freedom of speech and action allowed in Athens, that, although Socrates had for upwards of five-and-twenty years pursued his remarkable career, not until he had reached the age of seventy was any complaint publicly preferred against him. In no other ancient city would such a bold and independent course of action,

[1] Laws, 900–903. [2] Plat. Rep. 380 B. [3] Laws 904, 905.

running counter, as it did, to all established opinions, have been for so long a time tolerated.[1] "The envy and malice of the multitude," Socrates himself declares in the Apology, "is what will condemn me, if condemned I am."[2] That such feelings should have been aroused in by far the greater number of those brought in contact with him can hardly surprise any student of human nature; for his ironical and unsparing cross-examination, although conducted with great suavity and courteousness was yet calculated to excite the bitterness of wounded pride in any but an earnest seeker after truth. Doubtless, also, the people, still smarting under the recollection of the tyrannous oppression of the Thirty, resented his open confession of aristocratic tendencies; for, although studiously avoiding any part in public affairs, he never hesitated to declare his opinion of the way in which they were conducted, or to contrast the Athenian government with that of other states which approached more nearly his own ideal. Against the existing custom of electing magistrates by lot, his ridicule was especially directed. "No one," he says, "would be willing to choose a pilot by lot, or a smith, or a musician; and yet mistakes committed in any of these professions bring about far less harm than do mistakes committed in the service of the state."[3] We should have, however, anything but an adequate conception of the pure and patriotic wishes of Socrates for his country, if we understood him to attach real importance to any outward form of government. To him an aristocracy was essentially what the word in its original sense means, — the government of the best or worthiest. He declares that "the true kings and rulers

[1] See Grote's History of Greece, chap. lxviii.

[2] Apology, 28 A.

[3] Xen. Mem. i. 2, 9.

are not they who hold the sceptre, nor those chosen by any chance persons or elected by lot, nor yet those who have forced themselves into posts of command or obtained the same by wile; but they who know how to govern."[1] Socrates was also charged, though unjustly, with the political misconduct of Alcibiades and Critias, the two most hated names in Athens. They had, in early years, frequented his society, perhaps with a view to gaining facility in argument, and doubtless while they remained with him their vicious propensities were held in check. To this influence of Socrates Alcibiades is made to testify in the Symposium:—

"When we hear the words of any other orator, however eloquent, we remain comparatively indifferent to them; but when any one, be it man, woman, or child, hears you, or even your words through the mouth of another person, be he but an indifferent speaker, he is overpowered and, as it were, taken possession of by them. Indeed, friends, if I did not fear that I should appear to you to have been drinking, I would declare to you now, on oath, all I have felt and am still made to feel by the power of his words; for when I listen to him, my heart beats and tears come to my eyes, and I am more roused by far than are the Corybantian revellers in the rites of Cybele. And so it is, I see, with every one else. In listening to Pericles and other eloquent orators, I have thought that they spoke well; but never was I affected in this way, nor was my soul troubled and indignant at the thought that I was in a slavish condition. But I have often been put into such a state by this Marsyas, that it has seemed to me impossible to live as I am; and even now I am quite conscious that, if I should

[1] Xen. Mem. iii. 9, 10.

lend my ear, I should not be able to resist him, but should suffer again in the same way; for he compels me to acknowledge that, although I am far worse than I ought to be, I yet do not take care of my own soul, but busy myself with the affairs of the Athenians. Therefore, stopping my ears, as if to shut out the voice of Sirens, I tear myself away by force, lest I grow old sitting by his side. In his presence alone have I felt that which no one would suppose was in me to feel — shame. For while I am conscious that I cannot gainsay him or maintain that I ought not to do what he bids, still, as soon as I get away, the value I attach to popularity overcomes me. So I flee from him and make my escape; and when I see him, I am ashamed at what I have acknowledged to him. Many a time should I have been glad to know that he was no longer among men; and yet, had he died, I well know that this would have grieved me still more sorely, so that really I do not know what I am to do with the man."[1]

The trial of Socrates, perhaps the most momentous within the annals of history prior to the Christian era, took place before one of the popular tribunals, or Heliastic courts, composed of five hundred (or, more exactly, five hundred and one) members of the great body of six thousand judges chosen yearly to administer justice in Athens. His accusers, three in number, seem to have been men of no high character and of little renown, although Anytus, the most influential of the trio, had at that time attained to some political eminence. An Athenian trial presented a very different scene from that witnessed to-day in a court of law, resembling more nearly a scene before some tribunal of the French revolution.

[1] Plat. Sympos. 215, 216.

Of this we are kept in mind by frequent allusions in the Apology to continual interruptions and disturbances, for the hall was crowded by spectators, who gave vent to the various feelings aroused by the speaker, in loud murmurs or groans. It was customary also for the dikasts, or jurors, to interrupt the speaker by questions and remarks, and sometimes the parties to the suit would engage in discussion with each other, as we gather from the amusing little episode of the discomfiture of Meletus.[1]

It is difficult to determine with absolute certainty how close a relation the Apology, as reported by Plato, bears to the exact words spoken by Socrates; but in the opinion of Grote and other authorities, it is "in substance the real defence; reported, and of course drest up, yet not intentionally transformed, by Plato."[2]

"No one," says Grote, "who reads the Platonic Apology of Socrates will even wish that he had made any other defence. But it is the speech of one who deliberately foregoes the immediate purpose of a defence, — persuasion of his judges; who speaks for posterity without regard to his own life. I have already remarked, in reference to his trial, that, considering the number of personal enemies whom he made, the wonder is not that he was tried at all, but that he was not tried until so late in his life. I now remark, in reference to the verdict, that, considering his speech before the dikastery, we cannot be surprised that he was found guilty, but only that such a verdict passed by so small a majority."[3] There can be little doubt indeed that, had he chosen to adopt a more conciliatory tone towards his judges, the sentence would have been a very different one, if indeed he had been

[1] Apology, 24 E to 28. [3] Grote's History of Greece, chap. lxviii

[2] Grote's Plato, chap. vii.

condemned at all. "But he was not willing to do any of those things contrary to law which are wont to be done in court; and although had he consented to do anything of the kind, even in a very moderate degree, he might easily have got from the judges his release, he preferred to die abiding by the laws, rather than transgressing them to live."[1]

The last scene in the prison of Socrates, as recorded in the Phaedo, forms a fitting close to a life so long devoted to the task of inspiring in others the same high hopes and aims by which he had himself been animated. In his dying request is embodied the great principle of immortality, meet subject for a philosopher's last words. Exultant in the belief that through death the true life of health and activity was just opening before him, he desired to present a sacrifice of praise and thanksgiving, not only to the God of Health, but through and beyond him to the supreme Healer and Restorer of Life.

[1] Xen. Mem. iv. 4, 4.

CONTENTS

THE
APOLOGY OF SOCRATES

APOLOGY.

17 I KNOW not, O men of Athens, how you have been affected by my accusers, but I for my part, I assure you, scarcely recognized myself, so plausibly did they speak; and yet, not one word of truth, I may say, have they uttered. But among their many falsehoods, there was one at which I marvelled most of all: it was where they said that I was an eloquent speaker, and that you must therefore take care not to be led astray by me. That they were not ashamed to make this assertion, when they knew that it was on the very point of being refuted by me, is, I think, the most shameless part of the whole thing; for it will soon be apparent that I am not in the least an eloquent speaker, unless perchance they call him eloquent who simply speaks the truth. If that indeed be what they mean, I should be willing to confess myself an orator, though not one after their fashion. These men, then, as I was saying, have spoken hardly one word of truth; but from me you shall hear the whole truth, yet not, by Zeus, O

men of Athens, dressed up in finely worded speeches like their own, with figures and phrases and embellishments. No, indeed! you shall hear it plainly stated, in the first words that occur to me; and let none of you expect anything more than this from me, for I rely solely upon the justice of my cause. And certainly, citizens, it would ill become me, at my age, to appear before you like a boy with a carefully prepared speech. But this, above all, men of Athens, I beg and implore: if you hear me defend myself in the same words that I have been accustomed to use in the market-place, at the counters of the money-changers, where many of you have heard me, and in other places, do not be surprised, nor interrupt by raising a disturbance. For the matter stands thus. At the age of more than seventy years, I am now for the first time appearing before a court of justice, so that I am an utter stranger to the manner of speaking here. Therefore, just as you would doubt-
18 less pardon me, if I were in reality a stranger, for speaking in that dialect and fashion which I had been brought up to use, even so now I ask this justice — for such it seems to me — at your hands: that you disregard my manner, whether it be better or worse, and consider this alone, and to this turn your whole attention, whether I speak what is just or not. For this is the virtue of a judge, and to speak the truth is that of an orator.

First then, men of Athens, I am bound to answer my former accusers and the first false charges which were brought against me, and then the later charges and the last accusers. For my accusers are many in number, and it is a long time now — many years, in fact — that they have been speaking falsely against me. These I fear more than Anytus and his friends, although they are formidable enough; but those, fellow-citizens, are more formidable, who, getting hold of you for the most part while you were yet children, have persuaded you to believe this false accusation, that there is a certain Socrates, a wise man, who speculates on things in the heavens, and searches into all things under the earth, and makes the worse appear the better reason. They, O Athenians, who have spread this report are my really formidable accusers, for their hearers suppose that men who search into such things as these do not believe even in Gods. Then, too, these accusers are many, and have been bringing charges against me for a long time, and presenting them to you moreover, at that age — either childhood or extreme youth — when you were most easy to be persuaded; appearing, in fact, like plaintiffs in court with no defendant present. But the most senseless thing about it all is that we are not able even to find out who they are, or to call them by name, unless some one among them happens to be a comic poet. All those who from envy and malice, tried to mislead you, as well as those who urged upon you only what they themselves had been taught to believe, — all these, I say, are very hard to deal with, for it is impossible to summon any one of them here as a witness, or to question him. I must needs in defending myself fight, as it were, with shadows and question with no one to answer.

Assume with me, then, that, as I say, my accusers are of two classes, namely, those who of late have attacked me, and those old accusers of whom I have just spoken; and you will agree, I think, that I ought first to defend myself against the latter. For these you first heard accuse me, and much oftener too than those who came afterwards. This then is agreed. And so, Athenian citizens, I must
19 needs make my defence, and try to do away in so short a time with the bad opinion of me at which you have been arriving for so long a time. I could wish, indeed, if it were best for you as well as for me, that such might be the result, and that I might gain favour with you by my defence. But success, I think, will be difficult; how difficult, I do not conceal from myself. Let it so be, however, as God pleases; the law must be obeyed, and I must make my defence.

Let us therefore consider, from the beginning, what the charge is which gave rise to these slanders, and on which Meletus, you see, was relying when he brought this indictment against me. Well, then, in what words did my calum niators slander me? Let us read out their charge, as if it were a formal accusation made in court. "Socrates is guilty of crime, in that he busies himself with prying into things under the earth and in the heavens, and making the worse appear the better reason, and teaching the same to others."

This is the kind of charge; and this is what you yourselves have seen in the comedy of Aristophanes, where a certain Socrates appears wandering round, asserting that he walks the air, and babbling many other follies, about which I confess that I understand absolutely nothing at all. Now I do not mean to speak slightingly of this kind of knowledge, if any one really possesses it; may I never be brought to trial by Meletus on so heavy a charge as that! But really, Athenians, I have nothing to do with these matters. As witnesses to this, I summon the greater part of you here present, and demand that all who have listened to my discourses shall speak out and inform one another. There must be many such persons here. If any of you, then, have ever heard me say either much or little about such matters, tell it now one to the other. The result of this experiment shows you that the other stories which are told about me are of the same stamp.

Nor is the report true, which you may have heard, that I undertake to teach men and charge

fees for my instruction; there is not a word of truth in it. And yet this, I think, is a noble thing to do, if one is really capable of teaching men, like Gorgias of Leontini, and Prodicus of Ceos, and Hippias of Elis. For each one of these is able to go to any of our cities he pleases, and persuade our young men to forsake the so-
20 ciety of their own fellow-citizens, which they could have had without expense, and flock to him, and not only pay him money, but feel grateful besides. And there is another philosopher, a Parian, of whose arrival here I heard in this way: I happened to meet a man who has spent more money on Sophists than have all others put together, Callias, the son of Hipponicus, and knowing that he had two sons, "Callias," said I, "if your sons were colts or calves, we should be able to find some master, probably some horse-trainer or farmer, whom we could hire to bring out and improve the good qualities of their nature. But now, seeing they are human beings, what master have you in view for them? Who understands those good qualities which belong to the man and citizen? I ask you, because I suppose that, having sons, you have considered the matter. Is there any such person," I asked, "or not?"

"Certainly there is," he answered.

"Who is he?" I asked. "Whence does he come, and what is his fee for teaching?"

"Evenus, O Socrates," he answered. "He

comes from Paros, and he charges five minas." And I thought to myself that Evenus was a happy man, if he did in truth possess this art and teach it for so modest a fee. I assure you that if I had understood all this, I should have prided myself upon it, and given myself airs. But I really do not understand it, O Athenians.

And here some one of you may turn upon me, and say, "But, Socrates, what is it, then, that you are in the habit of doing? What is the origin of these slanders? For surely all this talk and this evil report about you did not arise while you, like the generality of people, were busying yourself about nothing unusual, and behaving in no wise differently from others. Tell us, then, what it is, that we may not give a rash judgment about you."

Now it seems to me that this is a very proper question, and I will try to show you what it is that has brought this name and this evil report upon me. Listen, then. And although some of you may think that I am in jest, I shall tell you the whole truth: be assured of that. I have obtained this name, O Athenian citizens, by reason of nothing but a certain kind of wisdom. "What kind?" do you ask? It is perhaps human wisdom, for in this I may, in reality, be said to be wise. The men, however, of whom I have just been speaking may turn out to have a kind of superhuman wisdom, — I really do not know what else to call it, as I, for my part,

do not pretend to understand it, and whoever says that I do, lies and seeks to slander me. And now, Athenians, do not interrupt, even if I seem to be talking extravagantly. The words which I am about to speak are not my own, but the speaker of them, to whom I shall refer you, is worthy of confidence. For to testify whether I have any wisdom, and of what kind it is, I shall summon the God of Delphi. You know
21 Chaerephon, I suppose. He was a friend of mine from childhood, and was also one of the associates in your democracy, for he shared in the recent exile, and returned from it with you. So of course you know what sort of a man Chaerephon was, and how eager in whatever he undertook. Well, once he went to Delphi, and had the boldness to consult the oracle about this matter. He asked, — I repeat, citizens, do not interrupt, — he asked if any one were wiser than I, and the Pythian priestess answered that there was no one wiser. To the truth of this his brother here will testify, as Chaerephon himself is dead.

Notice why I am telling you this. It is because I want to show you whence the calumny against me arose. Having heard the utterance of the oracle, I pondered in this wise: "How shall I explain the God's answer, and what does his riddle mean? I am not conscious that in me is any wisdom, whether great or small. What, then, can he mean by saying that I am the wisest of all men? I cannot suppose that he is speaking falsely, for that is not in the law of his nature." And for a long time I was at a loss as to what he meant, and then, after much hesitation, I set about my search in this way: I went to one of those who were reputed wise, thinking that there, if anywhere at all, I should be able to refute the oracle, and say to it, "You said I was the wisest man, yet here is one wiser than I am." But as I examined and conversed with him, — there is no need of my calling him by name, but, Athenian citizens, it was one of our statesmen with whom I had this experience, — it seemed to me that this man had the appearance of being wise in the eyes of many others, and most of all in his own, but in reality was not wise. Whereupon I tried to convince him that he only thought himself wise but was not really so, and consequently I became an object of hatred to him and to many of those who were present. And as I went away, I reasoned thus within myself: "I am wiser than this man; for it may well be that neither of us knows anything really beautiful and good, but he thinks that he knows something when he knows nothing, whereas I neither know nor think that I know anything. I do therefore seem to be wiser than he, at least in this small particular, that what I know not, I do not even think I know." Thereupon I went to one of those who had the reputation of being even wiser than this man, and here it was the same thing over again. And so I incurred his hatred too, and that of many others.

After this, I went to many in turn, perceiving with grief and anxiety that I was making myself hated, but nevertheless under the necessity, so it seemed to me, of making the will of God my first object. Now, in order to find out the meaning of the oracle, I had to seek all those who had the reputation of knowing anything; and, by the Dog, Athenians! — for I
22 must tell you the truth, — I swear to you that
this was my experience. Those in best repute seemed to me, in my divinely appointed search, not far from the most deficient; while others, held to be inferior, were really superior, so far as wisdom was concerned. And now I must tell you the tale of my wanderings; for I went through what I may call real labours that the oracle might be proved beyond question true. From the statesmen, then, I went to the poets, the authors of tragedies and dithyrambics, and all the others, thinking that here I must detect myself in the very act of knowing less than they. Taking, therefore, such of their poems as seemed to me the most elaborated, I would ask what was their meaning, in the hope that together with this I might obtain from them some other knowledge. Now I am ashamed to tell you the truth, citizens, and yet it must be declared; nearly all the bystanders, I may say

used to talk better than these very poets did about what they themselves had written. So much, then, about the poets I learnt in a short time: that what they did was done not by the help of wisdom, but by a certain natural gift and inspiration, just as the soothsayers and diviners say many beautiful things, of which, however, they understand not a word. Under some such spell as this, it appeared to me, were the poets; and yet at the same time, because of their poetry, they thought themselves, I perceived, the wisest of men in regard to other things, as to which they were not at all wise. So I went away, thinking that I was superior to them also just as I was to the politicians.

Finally I went to the artisans; for here I was conscious that I knew nothing, so to speak, while I was sure that I should find them versed in much that was beautiful. And herein I was not mistaken, for they knew what I did not know, and were in so far wiser than I. But it seemed to me, Athenian citizens, that the good artisans made just the same mistake as the poets. Each, because he worked well in his own art, thought himself wisest as to matters of another and a higher nature, and this error obscured the knowledge that he really possessed. So that when I asked myself, in the name of the oracle, whether I should be content to be as I am, neither wise with their wisdom nor ignorant with their ignorance, or else, like them, to possess both together, the answer which I made to myself and to the oracle was, "It is better for me to be as I am."

In consequence, Athenian citizens, of this in-
23 vestigation, much hatred has been engendered against me, so fierce and bitter that it has given rise to many slanders; and through this I have also got the name of being a wise man. For the bystanders always think that I am wise about those subjects on which I expose the ignorance of another. But the truth probably is, citizens, that it is the God who is really wise, and that he means in this oracle to say that human wisdom is worth little or nothing. And although he seems to be speaking of Socrates, he is only making use of my name, and holding me up as an example, as if he were saying, "He is wisest among you, O citizens, who, like Socrates, has come to know that he is in truth worth nothing as regards wisdom." I, therefore, still go about according to the God's command, examining and questioning any one who I think may be wise, whether citizen or stranger, and if it appears to me that he is not so, I make it known, and thus vindicate the oracle. And this occupation has left me leisure to do nothing worth speaking of, either in the state or for my own household, so that I am in very great poverty by reason of this my service to the God.

And yet again: those young men who have least to do, the sons of very wealthy persons,

follow me about without urging, and take pleasure in hearing these men cross-examined. They themselves, moreover, often imitate me, and undertake to examine others; finding indeed, I believe, no great scarcity of men who think they know something but really know little or nothing. Then those who have been cross-examined by them are angry with me, instead of being angry with themselves, and say that Socrates is a most pernicious fellow, and corrupts the young; but when they are asked in what way and by what teaching he does this, they have nothing to answer, because they do not know; that they may not appear, however, at a loss, they bring up the stock reproaches against all philosophers, that they tell of things in the heavens and under the earth, and teach men not to believe in Gods, and to make the worse appear the better reason. The truth, methinks, they would not wish to tell, — that they have been convicted of pretending to knowledge when they really know nothing. Since then they are, as I believe, many in number and ambitious and violent, and have been speaking against me plausibly and after a concerted plan, they have been filling your ears for a long time with their violent calumnies. And this is why Meletus and Anytus and Lycon have attacked me: Meletus being incensed on behalf of the poets, Anytus on that of the
24 artisans and politicians, and Lycon on account

of the orators; so that, as I said at first, I should be surprised if I were able, in this short time, to do away with a slander which has grown to be so great. This, O Athenian citizens, is the truth; and I tell it without concealing or suppressing anything, whether great or small. And yet I am well-nigh sure that it is this very frankness which makes me so hated; and this hatred, moreover, is a proof that I speak the truth, and that this is the cause of the calumny against me, and the ground of their prosecution; and if you will look into the matter, now or at any future time, you will find it to be so.

Let this, then, be a sufficient answer to the charges brought before you by my first accusers; I shall now try to defend myself against Meletus, the good man and the patriotic, as he calls himself, and against my later accusers. Let us next, therefore, take up the statement of their charge, as if they were a new set of accusers. It is, in substance, as follows: "Socrates is guilty, first, of corrupting the young, and, secondly, of not believing in the Gods acknowledged by the state, but in other new divinities." Such is the nature of the charge; and now let us examine each count in the indictment. It states, then, that I am guilty of corrupting the young: but I, O Athenians, state that Meletus himself is guilty; for he makes a jest of serious matters, bringing men lightly to trial, and pretending to be zealous and full of concern about matters to which he has never given a thought. That this is the real state of the case I will try to show you.

Come hither, Meletus, and tell me this. Have you not very much at heart that the young shall be as good as possible?

Mel. Certainly I have.

Socr. Well, then, tell the court who it is that makes them better. This, of course, you must know; it is your business, for you it is who have discovered me, you say, to be their corrupter, and have brought me here, and accused me before this tribunal. Speak up, then, and tell us who it is that improves them. Do you not see, Meletus, that you are silent, and have nothing to say? And yet is not this silence shameful, and a sufficient proof, moreover, of just what I say, that you have never given a thought to these things? But tell us, my good friend, who does improve the young?

Mel. The laws.

Socr. But, my excellent sir, what I asked was not this, but who the man is; and he of course, to begin with, must know these very laws of which you speak.

Mel. These judges here, Socrates.

Socr. What do you mean, Meletus? Are they able to train up the young, and do they improve them?

Mel. Certainly.

Socr. All of them, or only some and not others?

Mel. All.

25 *Socr.* By Here this is good news that you bring us! We have no lack of benefactors, then. And who besides? Do these bystanders improve them, or not?

Mel. Yes, they also.

Socr. And the senators?

Mel. The senators, as well.

Socr. But is it possible, Meletus, that those who sit in the public assembly corrupt the young, or do not they all too improve them?

Mel. They too improve them.

Socr. It seems, then, that all Athenians, except myself, make the young good and virtuous, and that I alone corrupt them. Is this what you assert?

Mel. I assert it most emphatically.

Socr. You are laying a great misfortune at my door! But answer me this: do you think it true in regard to horses also, that all men improve and only one injures them? Or is it not rather, on the contrary, some one person, or at the most very few, — namely, horse-trainers, — who can improve horses, while most people, if they attempt to handle and break them into use, only do them harm? Is it not so, Meletus, in regard to horses and all other animals? It is, most assuredly, whether you and Anytus deny it or not. The young must be fortunate indeed, if only one person corrupts, while every one else improves them! But, Meletus, you have sufficiently proved that you never troubled yourself about the young; a sure sign of your indifference is that you care nothing about the matter for which you are prosecuting me.

Tell us further, Meletus, in the name of Zeus, whether it is better to live among good or bad citizens. Answer, my good friend, for it is no hard question that I am asking. Do not the bad always work harm against their neighbours, while the good work good?

Mel. Certainly.

Socr. And is there any one who prefers to be injured rather than benefited by those with whom he lives? Answer, my good sir, for the law requires you to answer. Is there any one who prefers being injured?

Mel. Certainly not.

Socr. Come, then, do you bring me here on the charge of intentionally or unintentionally corrupting the young and making them worse?

Mel. Intentionally, I say.

Socr. Why, how is this, Meletus? Are you at your age so much wiser than I at mine as to have already found out that the bad always work harm against those who are nearest them and the good work good, while I, on the other hand, have reached such depth of ignorance as not to know that, if through me one of my fel-

low-citizens becomes a knave, I am in danger of receiving some harm at his hands? Do you maintain that I voluntarily commit so great an injury? Of this, Meletus, you have convinced neither me nor, I think, any other hu-
26 man being. Either I do not corrupt men at all, or else I corrupt them involuntarily; so that in either case you lie. Now, if I do it involuntarily, it is not lawful to summon me here for involuntary offences of this kind, but you should take me apart to admonish and instruct me; since it is plain enough that if I learn better I shall leave off doing what I now do involuntarily. But you were unwilling to proceed thus, and, having shirked the duty of associating with me and instructing me, have brought me before this court, whither it is lawful to summon only those who need punishment, not those who need instruction.

But really, Athenian citizens, as I said before, it is clear enough that Meletus has never cared either much or little about these matters. Tell us, however, Meletus, in what way do you say that I corrupt the young? Is it, as is stated in the indictment which you brought against me, by teaching them not to believe in the Gods in whom the city believes, but in other new divinities? Is this the teaching by which you say I corrupt them?

Mel. Most emphatically I say it is this.

Socr. Then, Meletus, in the name of these

very Gods of whom we are now speaking, tell me and these others here still more plainly what you mean. For I cannot make out whether it is that I teach men to believe in certain Gods, —in which case I myself also must believe, and so do not offend by being an utter atheist, but only by believing in different Gods from those in which the state believes, — or whether you charge me with not believing in any Gods at all, and teaching the same to others.

Mel. That is what I say, that you do not believe in any Gods at all.

Socr. To what end, O wonderful Meletus, do you say this? Do I then not hold, with the rest of mankind, that the sun and moon are Gods?

Mel. No, by Zeus, judges, he does not, for he says that the sun is stone, and the moon earth.

Socr. Do you forget, friend Meletus, and imagine that it is Anaxagoras you are accusing; or do you hold these persons here present to be so stupid and so unversed in letters as not to know that these doctrines which you ascribe to me belong to Anaxagoras of Clazomenae, whose books are loaded with them? And the young men learn them from me, forsooth, when they can often hear them at the theatre, for the sum of a drachma at most, and can then laugh Socrates to scorn if he pretends that they are his own, — such singular doctrines too as these are! But tell me, in the name of Zeus, do you really think that I believe there is no God?

Mel. By Zeus I swear that you believe there is no God at all.

Socr. Nobody will believe that, Meletus, and I doubt whether you do yourself. It seems to me, Athenians, that this man is exceedingly insolent and unrestrained, and that he has framed this indictment in a spirit of sheer wantonness and youthful intemperance. He is like a man
27 who has made a mock-riddle, and is putting this question to himself: "Will the wise Socrates discover that I am jesting and contradicting myself in my words, or shall I be able to deceive him and my other hearers?" For it seems to me that he flatly contradicts himself in the indictment, very much as if he were to say, "Socrates is guilty of not believing in Gods, but of believing in Gods." And this is behaving like a person who is in jest.

Let us now examine together, citizens, what seems to me to be the absurdity in his statement. And do you, Meletus, answer me; and do you, Athenians, I pray, bear in mind what I asked of you in the beginning, — not to interrupt me if I speak after my accustomed fashion. Can any one, Meletus, believe in things relating to humanity, without believing in the existence of human beings? I wish he would answer, citizens, and not keep interrupting. Does any one believe that there can be things relating to horses, and yet no horses? or things relating to flute-playing, and yet no flute-players? No one does, O best of men; since you do not choose to answer, I myself will tell both you and all the others here present. But this you *must* answer. Is there any one who believes that there are things relating to divine beings, and yet no divine beings?

Mel. There is no one.

Socr. You delight me by giving an answer, albeit reluctantly, and only because you were compelled by the court. You confess, then, that I believe and teach that there are divine things; whether new or old, at all events in divine things I do believe, according to your own assertion, for to this you have sworn in your accusation. Now if I believe in divine things, it surely follows of necessity that I believe in divine beings. Is not this so? It is, indeed; for, as you do not answer, I assume you to have assented. Do we not regard divine beings (or demigods) as either Gods or the sons of Gods? Do you agree to this, or not?

Mel. Of course I do.

Socr. Well, as you admit that I believe in demigods, then, if demigods are in some sense Gods, here is my proof that you jest and speak in riddles: for you say, first, that I do not believe in Gods, and then that I do, since I believe in demigods. For, if the demigods are the ille

gitimate children of Gods, either by nymphs or by other mothers, as you know they do say is the case, what man could believe in the existence of the children of Gods without believing in the existence of Gods? It would be just as absurd as to believe that mules are the offspring of horses and asses, and yet not believe in the existence of horses and asses. Surely, Meletus, you can have framed such an indictment with no other motive than that of seeing how far you could venture with us, or else because you were at a loss for any true charge to prefer against me. But that you can persuade any human being who possesses the smallest grain of sense that the same person may believe in things pertaining to demigods and Gods, and yet at the same time in neither demigods nor Gods nor
28 heroes, of this there is no possibility.

But really, Athenian citizens, it seems to me that I do not need an elaborate defence to prove myself not guilty on the indictment brought against me by Meletus; what I have said may suffice. But the statement I made before, — that I am very much hated by many people, — this, you must know, is quite true, and this it is which will condemn me, if condemned I am, not Meletus, nor yet Anytus, but the malice and slander of the multitude. For this has destroyed many other good men, and will, I think, destroy many still; there is no danger that it will stop with me.

"But," some one perhaps may say, "are you not ashamed, Socrates, of having followed a pursuit on account of which you are now in danger of being put to death?" To such an one I might with good reason reply: "You say not well, my friend, if you think that a man who is good for anything at all ought to take into account the chances of living or dying, and not rather, when undertaking anything, to consider only whether it be right or wrong, and whether the work of a good or of a bad man. Why, according to your opinion, all the heroes who fell at Troy would be but sorry fellows, and especially the son of Thetis, who set danger at naught in comparison with enduring any disgrace; so that when his mother, who was a goddess, addressed him, all eager to slay Hector, in words, I think, somewhat to this effect · 'If thou, my son, avenge the death of thy companion Patroclus, and slay Hector, thou thyself must die; for thy own fate,' said she, 'awaits thee straightway after Hector,' he, having heard the prophecy, made light of death and danger, dreading far more than these the disgrace of living as a coward who had not avenged his friend. 'Let death come straightway,' he said, 'after I have punished the wrong-doer, so that I remain not here by the beaked ships, a laughing-stock and a useless burden of the earth.' Do you suppose that he thought of death and danger?"

Now, Athenians, this is the very truth. Wherever any one either stations himself because he thinks it right to be there, or is stationed by his commander, there, I think, ought he to remain and face danger, taking into account neither death nor anything else in comparison with disgrace.

It would be a strange act indeed on my part, O men of Athens, after my remaining in whatever post I was stationed by the leaders whom you had appointed over me, at Potidaea, Amphipolis, and Delium, and facing death like any other man, if, now that I am, as I think and believe, under orders from the God to pass my life in the pursuit of wisdom and in examining myself and others, — if now, I say, through fear
29 of death or any other evil, I were to desert my post! That would be strange conduct indeed, and then might I in truth be justly arraigned in court for not believing in the existence of Gods; for then should I be disobeying the oracle, and fearing death, and thinking myself wise when I was not. For to fear death, citizens, is nothing at all but to think you are wise when you are not wise, — to think you know what you do not know. For no one knows what death is, or whether it may not be the greatest of all goods to men; yet do they fear it, as if they knew it to be the greatest of evils; and what is this but the same old disgraceful ignorance, — that of thinking you know what you

do not know? Now I, citizens, do perhaps differ from most men in this respect, and if I might claim to be wiser than any one else it would be in this: that, not knowing much about the things of the world below, I am convinced that I do not know; but that it is wicked and shameful to do wrong and to disobey any one, whether God or man, who is better than yourself, this I do know. From fear, then, of those evils which I know to be evils, I would neither fear nor flee that which for aught I know may be a good. So that, if you were now to acquit me, in despite of Anytus, who has urged that either I ought not to have appeared here at all, or that, having appeared, I ought not by any possibility to escape death, and who has, moreover, assured you that, if I am let off now, your sons will all be utterly ruined by the practice of what Socrates teaches; and if, in acquitting me, you should say: "We will not put faith this time, O Socrates, in Anytus, but will let you go, on the condition, however, that you no longer spend your time in this search nor in the pursuit of wisdom, and that if you are caught doing either again you shall die,"—if, I say, you were to release me on these conditions, I should say to you, "Athenians, I love and cherish you, but I shall obey the God rather than you; and as long as I draw breath and have the strength, I shall never cease to follow philosophy, and to exhort and persuade any one of you whom I happen to

meet, saying, as is my wont: 'How is it, friend, that you, an Athenian, of the city greatest and of most repute for wisdom and power, are not ashamed to be taking thought for glory and honour, and for your possessions that they may become as great as possible, while you take neither thought nor heed for wisdom and truth and for your soul that it may become as good as possible?'". And if any one of you questions my word, and says that he does take heed for these things, I shall not at once send him away nor turn from him, but shall question, examine, and test him; and if it appears to me that he does not possess virtue, but only says that he does, I shall upbraid him for making least of what is worth most, and much more of what is
30 of less account. And this I shall do to whomsoever I come across, be he young or old, stranger or citizen; but especially to you, citizens, as ye are nearer of kin to me. For this, be assured, the God commands; and I believe that there has never yet been a greater good in the state than this my service to the God. For I do nothing but go about persuading you, both young and old, not to let your first thought be for your body or your possessions, nor to care for anything so earnestly as for your soul, that it may attain to the highest virtue; and maintaining that not from possessions does virtue come, but that from virtue do possessions and all other good things, both private and public

come to man. If by such discourse I corrupt the young, then this doctrine of mine must be harmful; and if any one asserts that I say any thing else than this, he is talking nonsense. "And, Athenians," I should go on to say, "either hearken to Anytus or not, and either acquit me or not; but understand that I shall never act differently, even if I have to die for it many times."

Do not interrupt, Athenians, but keep that promise which I asked of you, — not to interrupt, no matter what I say, but to listen; for I think that you will gain by listening. I am now going to tell you other things at which you will very likely raise a clamour; but do not so, I beg of you. You may be very sure that if you put to death such an one as I have just said I am, you will not injure me more than your own selves. Neither Meletus nor Anytus could injure me in the least: they have not the power; for it is not, I think, allowed by the law of God that a bad man should injure one better than himself. He may indeed put him to death or send him into exile or deprive him of civil rights, and these he, and perhaps some others, may think to be great evils. I myself do not think so, but I hold to be a much greater evil that which Anytus is now doing, — endeavouring to put a man to death unjustly. Wherefore, O men of Athens, I am far from defending myself for my own sake, as might be expected; but for your sake I do it, lest in condemning me

you err, by rejecting the gift which God offers you. For if you kill me, you will not readily find another such as I, who am, as it were, although the comparison may sound somewhat ridiculous, fastened upon the state by God like some gadfly upon a powerful, high-bred steed who has become sluggish by reason of his very size and needs to be aroused. And as such a gadfly does God seem to have fastened me upon the state; wherefore, besetting you every-
31 where the whole day long, I arouse and stir up and reproach each one of you. Such a man, citizens, you will not easily find again, and if you take my advice you will spare me. But perhaps, being irritated, as sleepy persons are when suddenly aroused, you may strike out at me, and, persuaded by Anytus, hastily put me to death; and then slumber tranquilly on for the rest of your days, unless, indeed, God should in his care for you send some one else to rouse you. And that I am such a gift of God to the state you can see from this my conduct; for it is not in the ordinary course of human nature that I should have been thus neglectful of my own affairs, and have suffered my household interests to be uncared for these many years, while I was continually busying myself with yours, going about to each one of you individually, like a father or an elder brother, and trying to persuade you to take thought for virtue. If, indeed, I had gained

anything by this, and had received pay for thus exhorting, I should have had some reason for it; but now you yourselves see that, although my accusers have so shamelessly made all these other charges against me, they have not reached such a height of impudence as to bring forward one witness to testify that I ever either received pay or asked for it. But I can bring forward, I think, a very sufficient witness that I am speaking the truth, namely, my poverty.

Perhaps, however, it may seem absurd that I go about in private, giving advice and busying myself about people's affairs in this way, and yet do not venture to come forward in your public assemblies and advise the state. But the reason is the one which you have often times and in many places heard me give,— that there comes to me a something divine and spiritual, which Meletus indeed, by way of joke, has included in his indictment; and this is a voice which from childhood has frequently come to me, and which makes itself heard only to turn me back from what I am about to do, but never to impel me forward. This it is which stands in the way of my having anything to do with public affairs, and wisely, it seems to me, does it stand in the way; for you must know, O men of Athens, that if I had ever attempted to take part in the affairs of the state, I should long ago have perished, and thus have done no good either to you or to myself. Now do not

be angry with me for telling you the truth there lives not the man who would be safe in honestly opposing you or any other populace,
32 and in trying to prevent many unjust and unlawful things from taking place in the state; he therefore who is really fighting for the right must, if he would be safe even for a short time, lead a private life, not a public one.

I will give you full proof of this, not in words, but in deeds, which you value more. Listen, then, to what has happened in my life, that you may know that to no man would I ever yield, through fear of death, against my sense of justice, even though by not yielding I might instantly perish. The story I am going to tell you is tedious, and in the style so often heard in courts of law, but it is nevertheless true.

I have never, Athenians, held any office in the state, except that I was once in the senate, and it so happened that our tribe (the Antiochian) had chief direction of state affairs on that occasion when the ten generals who had not picked up the men after the naval combat were brought to trial. You wished to try them all in a body, which was contrary to law, as you all afterwards admitted; but I then alone, out of the whole body of fifty Prytanes, was opposed to doing anything against the laws, and voted in the opposition. And though the speakers were all ready to lay an information against me or to arrest me summarily, and though you were all urging them on with shouts, I felt it my duty to brave the danger, with law and justice on my side, rather than to take part with you in counselling what was unjust, through fear of prison or death. And this happened when the city was still ruled by the democracy. But once, when the oligarchy was in power, the Thirty sent for me to the Rotunda, and commanded me to go with four others to Salamis, and bring Leon the Salaminian that he might be put to death. They had given many like commands to others, wishing to involve as many as possible in guilt. Then again, not by word but by deed, did I show that for death I cared not a whit, — if this expression be not too unmannerly, — but that not committing an unjust or unholy deed was what I cared for beyond all things else. That government, strong though it was, could not frighten me into doing anything unjust; and so, when we came out of the Rotunda, and the other four went to Salamis to bring Leon, I went back to my home. And on account of this I should perhaps have been put to death, had not the government of the Thirty soon afterwards been broken up. To the truth of all this many will testify.

Do you really think, then, that I could have lived so many years if I had led a public life, and, acting as an honest man, had stood by the right and held this, as I ought, above every

other consideration? Far from it, O Athenian citizens; nor could any other man. But you
33 will find that I have always been the same my whole life long, in public affairs, if I ever took any part in them, as well as in private, never making concessions to injustice to please any one at all, whether one of those whom my accusers call my disciples or anybody else. Now I have never been a teacher to any man, but if any one, whether young or old, wished to hear me speak while carrying out my mission, I never grudged him the opportunity. Nor is it my habit to discourse when I am paid, and refuse to discourse when I am not; but I hold myself ready to be questioned alike by rich and poor, or if any one prefers that I should question him, I let him first answer me and then hear what I have to say. And whether any of my hearers become better or worse, for that I cannot justly be made answerable, for I never promised any instruction whatever, neither have I ever taught in any way. If any one, therefore, says that he has ever learned or heard from me in private what I have not said before all other men, you may be sure that he is not speaking the truth.

But why is it, then, that certain people like to spend so much time in my company? You have heard already, O men of Athens, — I have told you the whole truth, — that they like to hear me examine those who think themselves

wise and are not; for this, after all, is far from unpleasing. But on me, as I have said, it has been enjoined by God thus to act, both by signs and dreams, and in every way in which the divine will ever imposed any duty at all upon man. This, O Athenians, is the truth, and it is easy to prove. For if I am corrupting some of the young men, and have corrupted others, surely some of those who are now grown up, and have come to know that when young they received bad advice from me, ought now to appear in court, in order to accuse me and have me punished. Or if they themselves were unwilling to do this, some of their kinsfolk, fathers, or brothers, or others belonging to them, should, if members of their family had received any harm at my hands, remember it now against me, and seek my punishment. Many such, I doubt not, are here present; indeed I see some of them at this moment. First, here is Crito, a man of my own time of life and from my own district, father of Critobulus here. Then Lysanias the Sphettian, father of Aeschines; and Antiphon the Cephisian, father of Epigenes. And I see others whose brothers have been much in my company: Nicostratus, son of Theosdotides and brother of Theodotus,—now Theodotus himself is dead, so that he cannot seek to stop him; and Paralus, son of Demodocus, whose brother was Theages. I see also Adi-
34 mantus, the son of Ariston, whose brother Plato

is present; and Aeantodorus, brother to Apollodorus here. And many others I might name to you, some one of whom Meletus ought by all means, in the course of his own argument, to have brought forward as witness against me; or, if he forgot it then, let him bring one forward now. I will give way. Let him speak out, if he have any such testimony. But you will find, citizens, that quite the contrary of this is true: all are ready to help me, the corrupter, the man who works evil to their kinsfolk, as say Meletus and Anytus. Now they who themselves have been corrupted might have some motive for coming to my assistance; but their relatives who have not been corrupted, and are now elderly men, — what other motive have they for helping me than the good and true one, that they know Meletus is lying, while I am speaking the truth?

Well, citizens, these facts and perhaps others of the same nature make up about all the defence which I can offer. But some one among you may be indignant with me when he calls to remembrance how he himself, when engaged in some trial of far less importance than this, has prayed and besought the judges with many tears, and tried to move them to pity by bringing into court his children and others of his kinsfolk, with friends in great numbers; whereas I shall do none of these things, and that too when I am, it would seem, in danger of the last

penalty. Very likely some judge who calls this to mind may harden himself against me, and so, goaded by the recollection, may cast his vote in anger. Now if this be the case with any of you,—I do not assert that it is, but if it be,—it seems to me that I can say with rea son to such an one: "My friend, I too hav kinsfolk, for even as Homer says, 'Not of wood nor of stone was I born, but of man.'" Thus I have kinsfolk, and moreover, O men of Athens, I have three sons, one already a youth, two who are yet children. Not one of these, nevertheless, shall I bring here to implore you for my acquittal. And why will I do none of these things? It is not that I am self-willed, O men of Athens, or that I am wanting in respect to you, and whether I am courageous or not in facing death is another question; but as regards my own credit and yours, and that of the state, it does not seem honourable for me to do anything of the kind, especially at my age, and with the sort of reputation—whether true or false—that I have. For the world, at all events, has made up its mind that Socrates surpasses,
35 in some way, most other men. Now it would be a shame if those among you who are held to surpass others, either in wisdom or in manliness or in any other virtue, were to behave so unworthily. I have often seen men of good reputation behave strangely enough when brought to trial. They seemed to think that

in dying they were to suffer something strange and terrible, as though they expected to be immortal if not put to death by you. Such men, methinks, fasten disgrace upon the state, insomuch that any stranger would assume that the most virtuous of the Athenians, those who are picked out by their own fellow-citizens for posts of command and other honours, are in no wise better than women. But you, O men of Athens, those of you who have any reputation at all to lose, ought not thus to behave, nor should you suffer such behaviour in us. You ought to show that you will condemn the man who makes the city ridiculous by enacting such pitiable scenes, rather than him who keeps a quiet mind.

But putting aside, citizens, the discredit of the thing, it does not seem to me right either to owe one's escape to entreaties, or to supplicate a judge rather than to enlighten and convince him. For the judge sits in court to give judgment, not to award justice by favour; and he has not sworn to grant favours to whomsoever he pleases, but to judge according to the laws. It behooves us therefore not to accustom you to swear falsely, nor should you accustom yourselves to this, for in so doing, we should neither of us be acting with piety. Do not therefore claim, O men of Athens, that where you are concerned I ought to act in a way which I believe to be neither good nor just nor holy, above all, by Zeus, at the very time that I am under a charge of impiety made by this man, Meletus. For if I were to persuade you and by force of entreaties overpower your oaths, I should clearly be teaching you not to believe in Gods, and accusing myself of not believing in them while in the very act of defending myself against this accusation. But far from this, O men of Athens, I do believe in them as does not one of my accusers; and to you and to God I leave it to judge my case as shall be best for me as well as for yourselves.

Here follows an interval, in which the judges retire to vote upon the question of the guilt of Socrates. They announce, upon their return, a majority of about sixty votes against him; the penalty of death is proposed by his adversary Meletus, and it is now the turn of Socrates to propose a counter-penalty. He proceeds thus:—

I do not feel aggrieved, O men of Athens, at the sentence you have just pronounced against
36 me, and for this there are many reasons. The result was not at all unexpected, and I wonder only at the relative numbers of the votes. For I had thought that the majority against me would be not small, but very large; and now, as it appears, if only thirty of the votes had been changed to the other side, I should have been acquitted. And even now I may say that I have been acquitted, so far as Meletus is concerned; and not only this, but it must be evident to all that if

Anytus and Lycon had not joined him in accusing me, he would have failed to receive a fifth part of the votes, and so been fined a thousand drachmas.

The man, then, proposes for me the penalty of death. So be it. And what counter-penalty, O men of Athens, shall I propose to you for myself? Clearly one according to my deserts, must I not? What, then, shall it be? What do I deserve to suffer or to pay for my offence? You know what this is. My life throughout, I allowed myself no rest, but neglected what most men prize, money-making, family interests, military commands, public speaking, and all offices of the state, as well as plots and factions, deeming myself in truth too good a man to be safe if I entered into such things. I did not go where I could be of no use either to you or to myself, but wherever I thought I could do most good to each one of you in private, thither I went, and tried to persuade each one of you not to take thought for his interests before he had taken thought how he might improve himself to the utmost in virtue and in wisdom; nor for the interests of the state before taking thought for the state itself; and in all other concerns to proceed in the same way. What then do I, such a man as I have told you I am, deserve to receive? Some good, O men of Athens, at least if the penalty be fixed according to my real desert; and it should be a

good, moreover, that strictly befits me. What, then, does befit a man — poor indeed, but your benefactor — who needs leisure that he may use it in exhorting you? Nothing better befits such a man, O Athenians, than to be maintained in the Prytaneum at public expense. He deserves this surely far more than does one who has gained a prize at Olympia in a horse or chariot race. For he may cause you to appear happy, but I cause you to be happy; he needs not to be maintained, but I do need it. If, then, I am to propose a penalty according to my just
37 deserts, it shall be this, — maintenance in the Prytaneum.

Perhaps in saying this I may seem to be speaking defiantly, just as in what I said about the weeping and supplication. But this is not so, O Athenians. I speak thus, because I am fully persuaded that I have intentionally injured no man. You, however, I cannot convince of this, for it is but a short time that we have had to talk together. I think, indeed, that were it the law here, as in other countries, that capital trials should occupy not one day only, but several, I should have been able to convince you; but it is not easy in a short time to do away with great slanders. Being fully persuaded, however, that I have done no injury to any one else, far be it from me to do myself the injury of declaring that I deserve any evil, and of proposing any such penalty. What fear should induce me to do it? The fear lest I may suffer the penalty proposed for me by Meletus, of which I declare that I do not know whether it be a good or an evil? Shall I choose instead something which I know certainly to be an evil, and propose this for my penalty? Imprisonment? And why should I wish to live in prison, a slave to the magistrates who may happen to be in authority? Or a fine, and imprisonment until I shall have paid it? But in my case that would be neither more nor less than imprisonment, for I have no money to pay it. Shall I say exile, then?—for likely enough you would accept this penalty. I must be fond of life indeed, if I am so blind to reason as not to foresee that, since you, my own fellow-citizens, have not been able to bear my discourses and arguments, which have become so burdensome and hateful to you that you are now seeking to get rid of them, it is not likely that others will bear them more readily. Far from it, Athenians! Truly my life would be a pleasant one, if I should go into exile at my age, and be compelled to perpetually change my abode and flee from one city to another. For I know full well that, wherever I go, the young men will hearken to me, as they do here; and if I repel them they themselves will persuade their elders to send me away, while if I do not repel them their fathers and kinsfolk will send me away on their account.

"But, Socrates," some one may say, "if you will only keep quiet and hold your peace, can you not take yourself off and live somewhere else?" Now, to make certain among you understand this, is hardest of all; for if I tell you that it would be disobeying the God, and that for this reason it is impossible for me to keep quiet, you will think that I am not in earnest,
38 and will not believe me. Or, again, if I say that the greatest good to man is to discourse daily about virtue and those other matters about which you have heard me speak and examine both myself and others, and that a life without examination is not worth living, you will be still less likely to believe me. Yet, citizens, I tell you that these are truths, hard though it be to convince you of it. Furthermore, I am not accustomed to think that I deserve any punishment at all. If, indeed, I had the money, I might have proposed such a fine as I could have paid, for this would not have harmed me. But as it is, that is out of the question, unless, indeed, you are willing to make my fine so small that I shall be able to pay it. I might possibly pay one mina of silver; therefore I propose that amount. But Plato here, O men of Athens, and Crito and Critobulus and Apollodorus bid me say thirty minas, and offer to be my sureties. This, then, I propose; and for the payment of the money they will be ample security to you.

The vote of the judges is now taken upon the two penalties proposed by accuser and accused, and a majority is found to be in favour of the former. The trial is now ended, but Socrates avails himself of the short pause which elapses before his removal to prison to address his judges as follows: —

It is not much time, O men of Athens, that you will gain by shortening my life, in return for the evil name and the charge of having put to death Socrates, a wise man, which those who wish to speak ill of the city will fasten upon you. For those who wish to upbraid you will call me wise, even though I be not so. Now, if you had waited but a little while, what you wish would have happened in the natural course of events; for you see my time of life, how far on in years I am, how near to death! I say this not to all of you, but only to those who have cast their votes for my death. And this also I wish to say to these same men: You probably think, O citizens, that I have been convicted for the lack of such arguments as might have persuaded you, if I had thought it right to do or say every kind of thing in order to escape this sentence. Far from it. I have been convicted by a lack, not of arguments, but of audacity and of shamelessness, and of willingness to say such things as you would have liked to hear; because I would not weep and lament, and do and say many other things to which, indeed, you are accustomed in others, but which, as I have told

you, would be unworthy of me. But I did not then think that, on account of danger, I ought to do anything unmanly, nor do I now repent the manner of my defence. I would much rather die, having thus defended myself, than live on such terms as those. For neither in a court of justice nor in war ought I or any
39 other man to use every possible device whereby to escape death. In battle it often happens that a man may save his life by throwing down his arms and turning in supplication to his pursuers; and in all kinds of dangers there are many like devices whereby death may be avoided, if a man be willing to do and say anything whatsoever to that end. But I suspect, ye citizens, that the difficulty is not in escaping death, but much rather in escaping evil, for this runs faster than death. Now I, being slow and old, am overtaken by death, the slower; and my accusers, being swift and skilful, by evil, the swifter of the two. And now I go away condemned by you to receive the penalty of death; but they go condemned by truth to receive the penalty of wickedness and wrong. I must abide by my sentence, they by theirs. These things, peradventure, were destined so to be, and I believe they are for the best.

And now, O ye who have voted against me, to you I desire to prophesy concerning the future. For I have now reached that moment wherein men are most gifted with prophetic power, — the moment when they are about to die. I tell you, O ye citizens who have condemned me, that immediately after my death a punishment shall come upon you much severer, by Zeus, than that to which you have sentenced me. You have acted thus, thinking to be set free for the future from rendering any account of your lives; but I declare to you that the reverse of this will come to pass. Greater still will be the number of men who will cross-examine you, — men whom I have thus far held back, so that you have not perceived their existence; and the younger they are, the more severe they will be and the more you will be harassed by them. For if you think that by putting men to death you will hinder anybody from casting reproaches upon you for not living righteously, you are mistaken. That way of escape is by no means a possible or an honourable one; but this one is not only most honourable but most easy, not to restrain others, but to endeavour yourselves to grow in all virtue. Thus having prophesied to you who have condemned me, my part with you is done.

And now I turn to you who have voted in favour of my acquittal, for I would gladly talk with you of this thing that has just happened, while the officers are otherwise busied, and before I go to the place where I am to die. I pray you, then, my friends, stay with me yet this space of time, for nothing prevents our talking

with one another as long as we are permitted.
40 To you, knowing that you are my friends, I wish to unfold the meaning of this which has now befallen me. For to me, O my judges,— and in calling *you* judges, I name you indeed rightly,—a wonderful thing has happened. The accustomed prophetic sign of my divine monitor has hitherto ever constantly opposed me even in the merest trifles, if I were about to make a mistake. And now that which you yourselves have witnessed—the greatest of evils, as it might be and indeed is considered—has come upon me; yet not once, either as I left my house this morning, or on my way here to the court, or at any point in my argument, has the divine sign opposed me. And although on other occasions it has often cut me short in the midst of what I was saying, yet in this affair it has opposed me neither in my actions nor in my words. What do I take to be the reason of this? I will tell you. It must be that what has happened is for my good, and it is not possible that those of us who think death to be an evil are judging rightly. Of this what has happened seems to me a strong proof, for it is certain that the accustomed sign would have opposed me if I had not been on my way to my own good.

And now let us reason in this way, and we shall see what great hope there is that death is a good. For death must be one of two things:

either he who is dead becomes as naught, and has no consciousness of anything; or else, as men say, there is a certain change and a removal of the soul from this place to some other. Now if there be no consciousness, and death be like a sleep in which the sleeper has no dreams, then were it a wonderful gain indeed. For I think that if any one were called upon to single out that night in which he had slept so soundly as to have had no dreams at all, and, setting against it all the other nights and days of his life, to declare, after due thought, how many had been better and sweeter than that one, — I think, I say, that even the great King himself, not to speak of any private person, would find these so few in number that they might easily be counted in comparison with all the other days and nights of his life. If death, therefore, be such as this, I call it a gain; for all eternity, indeed, would thus appear no longer than a single night. But if, on the other hand, death be a transition to another place, and if it be true, as has been said, that all who have died are there, what, O judges, could be a greater good than
41 this? For if a man, being set free from those who call themselves judges here, is to find, on arriving in Hades, those true judges who are said to administer judgment in the unseen world, — Minos and Rhadamanthus and Aeacus and Triptolemus, and those other demigods who were just in this life, — will his transition

thither be for the worse? What would not any one of you give to converse with Orpheus and Musaeus and Hesiod and Homer? I, at least, would gladly die many times, if this be true; for to my thinking that state of being would be wonderful indeed, if in it I might have the chance of meeting with Palamedes and Ajax, the son of Telamon, and other heroes of the olden time who died through unrighteous judgment. To compare my own suffering with theirs were, methinks, no unpleasing task; but best of all would it be to examine and question there, as I have done here, and discover who is really wise, and who thinks himself so but is not. What, O judges, would a man not give to question him who led the great army against Troy, or Ulysses or Sisyphus or the thousand others, both men and women, whom one might mention? To dwell and converse with them and to question them would indeed be happiness unspeakable! For assuredly, in that world, at all events they do not put you to death for doing this; and not only in other things are they far happier than we here below, but, if what is said be true, they are there immortal for the rest of time.

But you too, O judges, it behooves to be of good hope about death, and to believe that this at least is true,— there can no evil befall a good man, whether he be alive or dead, nor are his affairs uncared for by the Gods. Neither has this

thing happened to me by chance, for I am persuaded that to die now and be released from worldly affairs is best for me, and that this is why the sign did not turn me back. Wherefore I bear no malice at all against my accusers or against those who have condemned me; but as it was not with this idea, but rather with the intent to do me injury, that they accused and voted against me, it is right that they should be blamed. This favour nevertheless I ask of them: When my sons are grown up, avenge yourselves, fellow-citizens, upon them, by tormenting them just as I have tormented you, if they appear to care for riches or for anything else above virtue; and if they pretend to be something when they are really nothing, then reproach them, as I have reproached you, with not caring for what they ought, and with thinking themselves to be something when they are
42 worth nothing at all. If you do this, I shall have received justice at your hands, — I, as well as my sons. But now it is time for us to go away, I to die, you to live. Which of us is going to the better fate is unknown to all save God.

CRITO.

CRITO.

The speakers are SOCRATES and CRITO.

The scene is in the prison of SOCRATES, *at Athens.*

CRITO.

43 *Socrates.* Why have you come at this time of day, Crito? Is it not still quite early?

Crito. It is early indeed.

S. About what time is it?

C. Day is just beginning to dawn.

S. I wonder that the keeper of the prison was willing to answer your knock.

C. He is used to me now, Socrates, I have been here so often; and besides, he has received some kindness at my hands.

S. Have you just come, or have you been here some time?

C. Some little time.

S. Then why did you not wake me up at once, instead of sitting by in silence?

C. By Zeus, O Socrates, I for my part should not have wished to be awakened to such a state of sleeplessness and sorrow. But I have for some time been looking at you with wonder to see you sleep so serenely; and I purposely did not awaken you, that you might pass the remainder of your time as peacefully as possible. Often before in the course of your life have I esteemed you fortunate in having such a nature, but never so much as now, in this present misfortune, seeing how easily and calmly you bear it.

S. But do you not see, Crito, that it would be quite inconsistent in one of my age to be disturbed at having to die now?

C. But when others, Socrates, of the same age are overtaken by like misfortunes, their age does not prevent their being distressed at the fate before them.

S. That is true. But why have you come so early?

C. To bring bad news, Socrates; though not for you, it seems. But for myself and for all your friends it is indeed bitter and grievous; and I, above all others, shall find it most hard to bear.

S. What is it? Has the ship come from Delos, on whose arrival I am to die?

C. She has not actually arrived, but I suppose she will be here to-day, to judge from tidings brought by certain persons who have just come from Sunium and report that they left her there. It is evident, from what they say, that she will be here to-day, and thus to-morrow, Socrates, your life must needs end.

S. But this, Crito, is for the best. If it please the Gods, so be it. I do not think, however, that the ship will arrive to-day.

44 *C.* Whence do you infer this?

S. I will tell you. I am to die on the morrow of the day on which the ship arrives.

C. So say they who order these things, you know.

S Well, then, I do not think she will arrive on this coming day, but on the following one. I infer this from a certain dream which I had this very night, only a little while ago. It was by some lucky chance that you did not awaken me earlier.

C. What was your dream?

S. It seemed to me that a woman in white raiment, graceful and fair to look upon, came towards me, and, calling me by name, said:—

"On the third day, Socrates, thou shalt reach the coast of fertile Phthia."

C. What a strange dream, Socrates!

S. But clear withal, Crito, it seems to me.

C. Only too clear. But, O beloved Socrates, be persuaded by me while there is yet time, and save yourself. For if you die, it will not be simply a misfortune to me, but, apart from my being deprived of such a friend as I shall never find again, it will appear to many, who know neither you nor me very well, that, al though it was in my power to save you had I been willing to spend money, I did not care to do so. And what imputation could be more shameful than that of valuing money more than friends? For the multitude will never believe that you were not willing to escape hence when we were eager to have you do so.

S. But why, dear Crito, do we care so much about the opinion of the multitude? Surely the most reasonable, those who are most worth considering, will believe that all has happened as it really has happened.

C. But do you not see that we must care about the opinion of the multitude? These very events now before us make it manifest that they are able to bring about not only the smallest evils, but the greatest, perhaps, of all, if any one is misrepresented to them by calumny.

S. Would that they were really capable, Crito, of bringing about the greatest evils, for then would they be capable of the greatest blessings also, and that were well indeed. But as it is, neither of these can they bring about; they are not able to make men either wise or foolish: whatever they do happens by chance.

C. This may be as you say. But tell me,
Socrates; you are not concerned, are you, with
regard to me and your other friends, lest, if
you escape, the informers may make trouble
for us as having stolen you away, and we be
made to forfeit all our property, or at least a
great deal of it, and perhaps suffer some other
45 evil besides? If it is, indeed, something of
that kind which you fear, make yourself easy,
for we should certainly do right in running this

risk, were it even greater than it is, in order to save you. So do not refuse to take my advice.

S I am concerned about this, and about many other things besides.

C. Now do not fear this, I beg of you; for the sum is not a large one, for the sake of which certain persons are willing to free you and conduct you hence. And do you not see how easily the informers are bought over?—so that we shall not need to spend much money on them. My own property is at your command, and is, I think, sufficient. But if, in your concern for me, you do not deem it right to make use of my property, here are friends from foreign parts, all ready to spend theirs. One indeed, Simmias the Theban, has brought for this very purpose a sufficient sum, and Cebes also and many others are holding themselves in readiness; so that, as I say, you must not refrain from saving yourself for fear of this. Nor let that of which you spoke in court be a difficulty to you, — that after leaving here you would not know what to do with yourself. For assuredly, wherever you go, there you will be beloved. If you wish to go to Thessaly, I have friends there who will make much of you, and afford you such security that none of the Thessalians shall in any way annoy you.

And moreover, Socrates, it does not seem to me that you are even acting justly, in giving yourself up when it is in your power to be

saved, for you are trying to bring the very thing upon yourself for which your enemies would strive, and for which they actually did strive in their desire to ruin you. And besides this, it seems to me that you are betraying your own sons, by forsaking them when it is in your power to bring them up and educate them; so that, as far as your help goes, their fate will be left to chance, and it will in all probability be that which usually befalls orphans in their bereavement. Either you ought not to have children, or, having them, you ought to endure the trouble of caring for and educating them to the end. You seem to me to have chosen what is easiest; whereas you ought to choose as would a good man and brave, especially one who had professed his whole life long to make virtue his chief care. For my part, I really am ashamed for you, and for ourselves, your friends, when I reflect that this whole case of yours may appear to have taken the turn it has by reason of some unmanly weakness on our part, which allowed the trial to come on when it might have been prevented, and to be conducted as it was in court; and the crowning absurdity of the whole is that now at the end, in our baseness and cowardice, we seem to have merely sought our own safety, taking no
46 more pains to save you than you did to save yourself, when we might easily have done so if we had been good for anything at all. See

to it, therefore, Socrates, that with this calam ity disgrace do not come upon us as well as upon you. Think it over; or rather there is no longer time for thinking, but your mind must be already made up. There is but one step to take. On this coming night all must be accomplished. If we delay in the least, it will be no longer possible. I beseech you, Socrates, be persuaded by me, and on no account refuse.

S. Your zeal, dear Crito, is worth much, if it be well-directed; but otherwise, the greater it is, the more dangerous. It behooves us then to consider whether this ought to be done or not. For I am now, as ever before, ready to be convinced by that argument alone which to my sober reason appears the most convincing. And now that this fate has come upon me, I cannot cast away the reasons which I gave in former times, for they still appear to me as good as ever, and I honour and reverence them just as I did before. Unless we can now find better ones, do not expect that I shall go over to your way of thinking, not even if the power of the multitude were to find still more bugbear terrors like the present ones, — imprisonment and death and loss of possessions, — wherewith to frighten us like children. How then may we most fairly look into the question? By taking up again that old argument about the opinions of men, to which you have just referred, and seeing

whether it is still true, as we used to maintain that we ought to pay attention to some and not to others; or whether, although this was true before my death was decreed, it has now become evident that it was a mere random saying, uttered only for the sake of talking, and was in reality mere childish nonsense. I wish to examine, Crito, together with you, whether the argument appears to me in a different light now that I am in this case, or whether it is still the same; and then we can either let it go or else abide by it. It has always been held, I believe, by those who profess to know anything, that, as I have just said, some men's opinions are to be had in honour, others' not. Tell me, by the Gods, Crito, does not this seem to you
47 well said? You, in all human probability, are not under the necessity of dying to-morrow, so that this present misfortune should not mislead you. Consider, then; does not this seem to you a satisfactory statement: that we are not to value all the opinions of men, but only some of them; and not those of all men either, but those of some only? Is not this well said?

C. It is.

S. And is it not the sound opinions we should value, rather than the worthless?

C. Yes.

S. And are not the opinions of the wise sound, and those of the foolish worthless?

C. How could it be otherwise?

S. Very well, and what was said before in regard to a like matter? Does a man, in training for the profession of gymnastics, pay attention to the praise and blame and opinion of all other men, or of the one only who happens to be his physician or trainer?

C. Of the one only.

S. He ought therefore to fear the censures and welcome the praises of this one person, and not those of the many.

C. That is plain enough.

S. Then he ought to act and exercise and eat and drink in the way which seems good to the one who understands and is a proficient, rather than in that approved of by all other men.

C. That is true.

S. Very good. If then, disobedient to the one, and dishonouring his opinion and approval, he honour that of the many who have no experience, will not harm come to him?

C. How could it be otherwise?

S. And what is the nature of this harm? Whither does it tend, and what part of the disobedient person does it affect?

C. Clearly it affects the body; for that is what it destroys.

S. True enough. Well then, Crito, in regard to other things, — not to go through with them all, in regard to the just and the unjust, the base and the beautiful, the good and the evil, on which we are now deliberating,—are we to fear and follow the opinion of the many, or that of the one man (if indeed there be such an one) who is wise as to these matters, and whom we ought to fear and reverence more than all the others put together, while, if we be not led by him, we shall corrupt and degrade that part of us which is made better by justice, but ruined by injustice? Is there not such a part?

C. I think there is, Socrates.

S. Well then, supposing, by not yielding to the opinion of the wise, we destroy utterly that part of us which is made better by health but corrupted by disease; is life worth living after this corruption has taken place? And that part is the body, is it not?

C. Yes.

S. And would life be worth living, with a miserable and corrupted body?

C. By no means.

S. But would it then be worth living, if that
part of us were corrupted which injustice de-
grades and justice benefits? Or do we indeed
hold that part, whatever it is, with which injus
48 tice and justice have to do, of less account than
the body?

C. By no means.

S. Of more importance then?

C. Of much more.

S. Then indeed, my friend, we ought not to heed at all what the multitude say of us, but only what the one man who understands about the just and the unjust, and what truth herself will say. So that, to start with, you do not state the case rightly in saying that we ought to give heed to the opinion of the multitude concerning the just and the honorable and the good and their opposites. "But," some one may say, "the multitude have power to put us to death."

C. Yes, and this is true enough. It might indeed be said, Socrates.

S. You speak truly; and yet, my excellent friend, this argument which we have been following out appears to me the same as ever. Now consider also whether we still hold that it is not mere living which should be valued above everything else, but living a good life.

C. Certainly we hold it.

S. And that living a good life is the same as living an honourable and a just life; do we still hold that or not?

C. We do.

S. Then, starting from these admissions, we must consider whether I should be acting justly or not in trying to escape when the Athenians refuse to release me; and if it appears that I should be acting justly, we will make the attempt; if not, we will renounce it. Those considerations of which you speak, concerning the loss of possessions and reputation, and the bringing up of children, belong, in truth, Crito, I fear, to those who thoughtlessly put men to death, and would as thoughtlessly bring them to life again if they could, with no reflection in either case; I mean that very multitude of which we have been speaking. But we, since our argument leaves us no escape, have, I think, no other question to consider than the one which we just now mentioned, — whether we shall be acting justly in bestowing money and thanks upon those who will get me out of this place, thus aiding and abetting our own escape, or whether in truth both we and they shall thus be doing anything unjust; and if it does appear that we shall thus be acting unjustly, we must not take into account the prospect of death if we remain quietly here, or of any other evil, in comparison with doing what is unjust.

C. What you say, Socrates, seems to me admirable; but what shall we do then?

S. Let us take counsel together, my friend, and if you have any objections to make to what I say, speak out, and you will find me ready to be convinced by you; but if you have not, pray, my good friend, no longer keep repeating this same thing, — that I ought to depart hence against the will of the Athenians, for I hold it of great moment to act in this matter with your approval and not without your consent Look then at the first step of our investigation, and see if it has been satisfactorily stated, and

49 then try to answer my question according to your real convictions.

C. I will certainly try.

S. Do we then hold that we ought in no way intentionally to commit injustice, or that we may commit it in one way, and not in another; or do we still, as in former times, admit that to act unjustly is in no case good and honourable? Are all the principles which we have acknowledged within these last few days to be now thrown away, and have we, Crito, at our age, been thus long and earnestly reasoning among ourselves, unconscious all the while that we were no better than children? Or rather, whether the mass of men acknowledge it or not, and whether a sterner or a milder fate is in store for us, is not what we said before still true, that to do injustice is in every way a disgrace and an evil to the doer of it? Do we admit this or not?

C. We do.

S. Then we ought not to do wrong at all.

C. Certainly not.

S. Nor should we, as the mass of men think, retaliate when unjustly treated, seeing that we ought never to commit any injustice at all.

C. So it appears.

S. How stands it then? Ought we to do harm to any man?

C. Of course we ought not, Socrates.

S. How then? Is it right, as the mass of

men assert, to render evil for evil, or is it not?

C. By no means.

S. Because doing harm to others is in no wise different from committing injustice.

C. You speak truly.

S. So that we ought neither to retaliate nor to harm any man, no matter what we may suffer at his hands. But look, Crito, at what you are hereby acknowledging, lest you unadvisedly admit something contrary to your real opinion; for this I know is believed and will be believed by very few, and they who do hold it and they who do not, have no common ground, but must of necessity despise each other, on account of their contrary opinions. Consider well, therefore, whether you agree with me and are of my mind; and then let us start with this conclusion, that it can never be right to commit injustice or to retaliate or to defend ourselves by rendering evil for evil. Or do you not agree to this first step, and will you give it up? To me it has always seemed and still seems true; but if you think otherwise, say so and instruct me. If, however, you do abide by it, listen to what follows.

C. I do accept it and abide by it. Say on.

S. I proceed then to tell you what follows from it; or rather, I will ask you to tell me. Ought a man to do what he acknowledges to be right, or ought he to betray the right?

C. He ought to do what is right.

S. Then notice how this applies. By going away without the consent of the state, shall we or shall we not be wronging those whom least of all we ought to wrong? And are we
50 thus abiding by what we acknowledge to be right, or not?

C. I have nothing to answer, Socrates, to what you ask, for I do not know.

S. Well, consider it thus. Suppose, as we were on the point of running away, or whatever else you may call it, the laws and the state should come and say: "Tell us, Socrates, what is this that you think of doing? Are you not, by the deed which you are about to undertake, thinking to destroy, so far as in you lies, the laws and the whole state? For you do not deem it possible, do you, that that state can survive and not be overthrown in which the decisions of the courts do not prevail, but are by private individuals set aside and brought to naught?" How shall we reply, Crito, to this, and to other like questions? Any one, above all an orator, might have much to say in behalf of the law we are breaking, which command that judgments once decreed shall be decisive. Or shall we make answer that the state has injured us and not given righteous judgment? Shall we say this, or what shall we say?

C. This, by Zeus, O Socrates.

S. What then, if the laws answer: "And

is this what was agreed between us, Socrates, or was it not rather that you should abide by the judgments decreed by the state?" And were we to express surprise at their speaking thus, they would very likely reply: "Do not be surprised, O Socrates, at what we say, but answer, since you are in the habit of asking and answering questions. Come then, what charge is it upon which you are trying to destroy us and the state? Did we not in the first place bring you into existence, and was it not by our authority that your father received your mother in marriage and gave you life? Tell us, therefore, is it those among us relating to marriage that you blame as not being right?" "I do not blame these," I should reply. "Is it then those relating to the nurture and training of children, under which you yourself were brought up? Are those laws among us, pray, not well-ordered which enjoined upon your father to instruct you in music and gymnastics?" "They are well-ordered," I should reply. "Very good. Having, therefore, been thus brought into existence and nurtured and educated, can you pretend to say that you are not our offspring and slave, you, even as were your fathers before you? And if this be so, do you think that your rights are equal with ours, and that whatever we undertake to do to you it is right for you to do to us in return? As regards your father or your master, if you chance to have one, your rights

are surely not equal. You would have no right to pay him back what he had made you suffer, whether by retaliating if he had abused you, or
51 by striking him if he had beaten you, or by doing anything else of the kind; and yet when it comes to us, your country and its laws, all this is allowable, forsooth, so that, if we have thought it right to undertake your ruin, you think yourself justified in doing in your turn all you can to bring about our destruction! And is this what you call acting justly, you who in very truth have made justice your special study? Are you so wise, pray, as to have missed the discovery that above your mother and father and all your other ancestors your country should be held in honour and reverence and holy awe, and is so held in the eyes of the Gods and of all reasonable men; that you must revere her and submit yourself to her, and soothe her in her anger more than if it were your father; that you must either induce her by persuasion to reverse her judgments, or else do whatever she commands; that you must suffer without resistance if she assigns to you suffering; and if she orders you to be scourged or imprisoned, or leads you into battle, there to be wounded or killed, that all this is right and must be done; that we must never give way nor retreat nor leave the ranks, but whether in battle or in a court of justice or anywhere else, we must either do what our

city and our country command, or else convince them of the true nature of justice? For it is impious to offer violence to your father or your mother; how much more, then, to your country!" What shall we say to this, Crito? Do the laws speak truly or not?

C. It seems to me that they do.

S. "Consider then, Socrates," the laws might continue, "whether we speak the truth in declaring that you are not treating us justly in attempting to do this thing. For we, having brought you into existence, nurtured, educated you, given you, as well as every other citizen, a share in all our good things, have moreover proclaimed to every Athenian, that after he has come of age, and examined our management of the city and ourselves, the laws, he has our permission, if he find that we do not please him, to take what belongs to him, and go wherever he wishes. And not one of us, the laws, hinders or dissuades any one of you, if we or the city do not please him, from taking his departure, if he wish, for one of our colonies, or from going to live in any foreign country that he may prefer, carrying with him all his possessions. But he among you who, having seen in what way we give judgment and manage the other affairs of the city, chooses to remain has, we assert, pledged himself, in very deed, to perform whatsoever we command; and him, if he does not obey us, we pronounce to be

thrice guilty: first, as disobedient to those who gave him being; secondly, as disobedient to those who brought him up; and thirdly, as neither obeying us when he has promised so to
52 do, nor trying to convince us if so be that we are in the wrong. And we do not harshly require obedience to our orders, but we lay open all questions for consideration; yet while we give him the choice of either convincing us or obeying us, he does neither of the two.

"To these charges, Socrates, we declare you liable, if you do what is now in your mind; and that not less but more than all the other Athenians." And if I were to ask why, they might retaliate, justly enough, by reminding me that I, of all the Athenians, had most pledged myself to this promise. "We have strong proofs, Socrates," they would say, "that we and the city itself have pleased you, for you would not have dwelt here more constantly than have all the other Athenians, if you had not been especially content. You never went out of the city at all, even to be a spectator at the games, except once to see the Isthmian; and you never went anywhere else, unless you happened to be serving in the army. Nor did you ever, like other men, travel abroad, nor desire to know about other cities or other laws, for we and our city satisfied you. Thus heartily did you prefer us, and pledge yourself to be governed by us; and besides, the fact that your children were born here is a proof that the city satisfies you. Moreover, in this very trial, you were at liberty, if you had wished, to propose the penalty of exile, so that what you are now attempting to do against the will of the city, you could then have done with her consent. You boasted at that time that if you had to die you would not be distressed, for you preferred, as you said, death to exile. But now you feel no shame at the recollection of your own words, nor have you any reverence for us, the laws, since you are trying to destroy us, and are acting as would the meanest slave, trying to run away in defiance of the covenants and agreements according to which you had pledged yourself to be governed as a citizen. Now, then, answer us this. Do we speak the truth in saying that you have pledged yourself to be governed by us, not in word, but in deed?" What shall we say to this, Crito? Can we do otherwise than acknowledge it?

C. We must needs do so, Socrates.

S. "Are you not then," they may say, "transgressing the covenants and agreements which were made with us, not by means of force or deception, nor yet because you were compelled to decide within a short time, for throughout the space of seventy years you were at liberty to go away if we did not please you, or if the agreements did not appear to you just. But you preferred neither Lacedaemon nor Crete,

which you often speak of as well governed
53 states, nor any other of the Greek or foreign
cities, and left Athens less frequently than do even the halt and the blind and the maimed; so much more than all other Athenians wer you satisfied with her, and, as naturally follows no less with us, her laws; for where is the man whom a city without laws would please? And now do you not intend to abide by your agreement? If you follow our advice, Socrates, you will, and not make yourself ridiculous by taking flight from the city.

"For just consider what good you will do yourself and your friends by setting at naught and violating these agreements. That your friends will be in danger of being exiled and deprived of their country and their property is well-nigh certain; and as to yourself, if you go to one of the nearest cities, — say Thebes or Megara, which are both well governed, — you will go as an enemy to its constitution, and those of its citizens who care for the state will look upon you with suspicion, as a subverter of the laws; and thus you will confirm the opinion of your judges, so that your sentence will appear to have been justly awarded. For whosoever is a corrupter of the laws is very sure to appear also as a corrupter of young and thoughtless men. Will you, then, flee from well governed cities, and from the men who are the most law-abiding? And if you must

do this, is it worth your while to live? Or if you can without shame associate with them, what language will you use, O Socrates? Will you affirm, as you have done here, that virtue and justice and institutions and laws are the things most precious to men? And do you not think that this deed committed by Socrates will appear unseemly? You must think so. But suppose you leave these cities, and go to the friends of Crito in Thessaly; for there reigns the greatest disorder and license, and they will very likely be glad to hear how ridiculously you ran away from prison in some disguise, perhaps clad in a leathern jerkin, or some other garment such as runaways are apt to wear, so that your whole semblance was changed. But do you imagine there will be nobody to relate how an old man, who has, in all probability, such a brief time remaining to live, was so greedy of life as to dare set at naught the highest laws? Perhaps not, if you do not offend any one; but if you do, you will be sure, O Socrates, to hear many disgraceful things said about yourself. You will live a slave and a mean flatterer to all sorts of men; and to what end withal, but to fare sumptuously, just as if you had taken your flight into Thessaly merely to get a dinner? And all those discourses concerning justice and other virtue — what is to become of them? Or is it per haps on account of your children that you wish
54 to live, so that you may bring them up and edu

cate them? But what then? Will you take them to Thessaly, and there bring them up and educate them, making them aliens to their country, that this also they may have to thank you for? Or perhaps you think that they will be better cared for and educated here in Athens for your being alive, even if you are not living with them? Your friends, you say, will look after them. But do you suppose that, while they will do this if you depart for Thessaly, they will not if you depart for Hades? Assuredly, if they who call themselves your friends are good for anything, you must believe that they will.

"But, Socrates, be persuaded by us who have brought you up, and do not place your children or your life or anything else above the right; that, when you have arrived in Hades, you may have all these things to urge in your defence before those who reign there. For neither in this life does it appear better or more just or more holy for you or for any one belonging to you thus to act, nor when you shall have arrived in the other world will it be to your advantage. As it is now, if you depart hence, you go as one wronged, not by us, the laws, but by men; but if you take to flight, thus disgracefully rendering back injustice and injury by breaking the covenants and agreements which you yourself made with us, and working evil against those whom least of all you ought to injure, — your own self as well as your friends, your country, and ourselves, — we shall be angry with you here while you are yet alive, and our brothers, the laws in Hades, will not receive you kindly, knowing that you sought, so far as in you lay to destroy us. So do not, we beg you, let Crito persuade you to follow his advice rather than ours."

These, you must know, my dear friend Crito, are the words which I seem to hear, even as the Corybantes imagine that they hear the sound of the flutes; and their echo resounding within me makes me unable to hear aught beside. Know, therefore, that if you say anything contrary to this, you will but speak in vain. Nevertheless, if you think that anything will be gained thereby, say on.

C. No, Socrates, I have nothing more to say.

S. Then so let it rest, Crito; and let us follow in this way, since in this way it is that God leads.

PHAEDO.

PHAEDO.

LIST OF SPEAKERS.

PHAEDO, *who repeats the dialogue to*
ECHECRATES.
SOCRATES.
CRITO.
SIMMIAS.
CEBES.
APOLLODORUS.
ATTENDANT OF THE PRISON.

The scene is in the prison of SOCRATES, *at Athens; and the dialogue is repeated at Phlius.*

PHAEDO.

57 *Ech.* Were you yourself, Phaedo, in the prison with Socrates on that day when he drank the poison, or did you hear about it from some one else?

Ph. I was there myself, Echecrates.

Ech. Then tell me, I pray you, what the man said before his death, and how he died? I would gladly hear. For none of our Phliasian citizens are at all in the habit now of visiting Athens, nor has any one for a long time come thence who could bring us any definite tidings of these things, excepting only that he drank the poison and died; but as to the rest, no one has been able to tell us anything.

58 *Ph.* Then you did not hear about the manner of his trial either?

Ech. Yes, some one did tell us about that: and we wondered why his death took place, as it appears, so long after the trial. Now why was this, Phaedo?

Ph. It came about by a special chance, Echecrates. It so happened that the stern of the ship which the Athenians send to Delos had been crowned the very day before the trial.

Ech. And what is this ship?

Ph. It is the ship, so say the Athenians, in which Theseus once embarked with those fourteen youths for Crete, and saved both their lives and his own. The people of Athens had, as the tale runs, made a vow to Apollo, that if these returned safely a sacred embassy should go forth every year to Delos; and from that time to this day it has yearly been sent in honour of the God. Now it is their custom, from the time the embassy begins, to keep the city pure and let no one die by the hands of the executioner until the ship shall have arrived at Delos and come back again, which may take a long time if it happens to be detained by contrary winds. The embassy begins as soon as the priest of Apollo has crowned the stern of the ship, and this, as I say, chanced to have been done the day before the trial. It was for this reason that Socrates was a long time in prison between his trial and his death.

Ech. And what about the death itself, Phaedo? What was said and done, and who of the man's friends were there? Or did not the magistrates allow any one to be present; and was he in his last hour alone, bereft of friends?

Ph. By no means: some of them were present; a goodly number, in fact.

Ech. Be good enough, then, to tell us all about

it as much in detail as you can; that is, if you do not happen to be in haste.

Ph. I am quite at leisure, and will try to go over it all; for to have Socrates brought to my mind, either by speaking of him myself or by listening to another, is of all things my greatest delight.

Ech. Why then indeed, Phaedo, you will have hearers of the same mind with yourself; so try to go over it all as minutely as you can.

Ph. I must confess that I had a strange feeling at being there. It was not pity that I felt, as when present at the death of a friend; for both from his manner and from his words, Echecrates, I deemed the man happy, and fearlessly and nobly did he meet death; so that I felt persuaded that even on his way to Hades
59 he went not without divine guidance, and that he would fare well when he arrived there, if ever man did. For this reason I felt no pity, as would have seemed natural at such a sorrowful scene. Nor yet did I feel pleasure, as we usually do in talking of philosophy, — for our conversation took somewhat that turn; what I experienced was something strange and unwonted, a feeling half pleasure and yet not unmixed with pain, as I reflected that he was about to die. And nearly all those present were affected in the same way, at one time laughing, at another weeping, one of us especially, Apollodorus. You know the man, of course, and his ways.

Ech. Why, certainly I do.

Ph. Well, he was wholly overcome; but I myself too was greatly moved, as indeed were all the others.

Ech. And who were the others, Phaedo, that chanced to be present?

Ph. Of his countrymen there was this same Apollodorus, and Critobulus, with his father Crito, and Hermogenes, and Epigenes, and Aeschines, and Antisthenes. And Ctesippus of the Paeanian deme, and Menexenus, and several others of his countrymen were there also. But Plato, I believe, was ill.

Ech. Were any strangers present?

Ph. Yes, Simmias the Theban, and Cebes, and Phaedonides; and from Megara, Euclides and Terpsion.

Ech. And how about Aristippus and Cleombrotus; were they there?

Ph. They were not; they were said to be in Aegina.

Ech. Well, was there any one else?

Ph. I think that these are about all who were there.

Ech. Go on then. What can you tell me of the conversation?

Ph. I will try to go over it all from the beginning. You must know, then, that I and the others had been in the habit, before this, of going daily to visit Socrates, assembling at dawn in the court-house where the trial had taken place, for it was near the prison. We used to remain there talking together until the prison was opened, which was not very early; and as soon as it was opened we used to go in to Socrates, and generally spent the day with him. But this time we had assembled earlie than usual: for the day before, on coming ou. of the prison at evening, we learned that the ship had arrived from Delos, and so we agreed among ourselves to come very early to the accustomed place of meeting. Upon our arrival, the door-keeper who usually answered our knock came out and told us to remain there and not go in until he should summon us.

"For," said he, "the Eleven are releasing Socrates from his bonds, and are bidding him be ready for death to-day."

We had not waited long, before he came back
and told us we might go in. On entering, we
60 found Socrates, who had just been set free from
his bonds, and Xanthippe, whom you know, sitting by, with his child in her arms.

As soon as Xanthippe saw us, she began to cry aloud and to utter such things as women are wont to do, as, —

"O Socrates, this is the last time that your friends will talk with you, and you with them."

And Socrates, turning to Crito, said: —

"Crito, let some one take her home."

So some of Crito's servants led her away, crying and beating her breast.

Then Socrates, sitting upright on the couch, bent his leg and rubbed it with his hand; and as he did so, he said: —

"How strange a thing, O friends, seems that which men call pleasure, and how wonderful a relation does it bear to what appears its very opposite, pain! They will never come together to a man; and yet if he pursue and catch the one, he is almost always forced to take the other also, just as if the two were joined together at one end.

"And I think," continued he, "that if Aesop had noticed this he would have made a fable out of it, that God, wishing to reconcile these two who were at enmity with each other, and not being able, had fastened their heads together, and that this is why, when one comes to a man, the other is sure to follow closely after. For even so seems it in my case, — whereas pain was caused in my leg by the chain, pleasure now seems to have come following close upon it."

"By Zeus, Socrates," here interposed Cebes, "you have done me a service by reminding me of something. Several persons have already questioned me about the poems which you have been composing, — those fables of Aesop which you put into metre, and the hymn to Apollo; and Evenus, only the other day, asked me what was your idea in writing them after coming here, when you had never written any poetry before

So, if you care for my having an answer to give Evenus when he asks me again, — for I know well enough he will, — tell me what I must say to him."

"Why, tell him the truth, Cebes," he answered, "that I did it, not with the wish to riva either himself or his poems, for I knew that was not easy; but I was trying to find out what could be the meaning of certain dreams I have had, and to clear myself from the sin of neglect in case this should be what they had meant by repeatedly enjoining upon me to cultivate the Muses. For their injunctions were in such wise: my whole life through the same dream has often come to me, sometimes in one shape, sometimes in another, but ever saying the same thing: 'Socrates, cultivate the Muses, and make this your work.' And I always supposed that it
61 was urging me on, as runners are urged on in a race, and encouraging me in what I was then doing, since philosophy is the highest province of the Muses, and I was engaged in its pursuit. But after the trial had taken place, and the feast of the God was delaying my death, I thought that the dream might possibly have meant, by its frequent admonitions, that I was to cultivate the Muses in this popular way; and if so, I ought not to disobey, but to do its bidding. For it seemed safer that I should not depart hence until I had atoned for my possible neglect and obeyed the dream by writing poems. First,

then, I composed a hymn to the God whose festival it was; but after this, remembering that a poet, if he have a mind to be a poet, must write not only truth, but fiction, and not being myself versed in story-telling, I took the fables of Aesop, which I knew well and had ready at hand, and turned into metre the first that came into my mind.

"This then, O Cebes, you can tell Evenus; and bid him farewell for me, and bid him also follow me as speedily as possible, if he be a wise man. I am to depart to-day, it seems, for so the Athenians have commanded."

Whereupon Simmias said:—

"What is this, Socrates, that you are urging upon Evenus? I have often met the man, and I am almost sure, from what I know of him, that he will not take your advice at all, if he can help it."

"What," said Socrates, "is not Evenus a philosopher?"

"I think so," said Simmias.

"Then Evenus, and every one else who takes a worthy part in this study, will wish to follow me. Very likely, however, he will not lay violent hands upon himself, for that, they say, is not lawful."

Saying this, he put his legs down from the couch to the ground, and sat thus during the rest of the conversation.

"But how," Cebes asked, "can you say that it

is not lawful to lay violent hands upon one's self, and yet that the philosopher will wish to follow the dying man?"

"What, Cebes, have not you and Simmias in your discourses with Philolaus heard all about these matters?"

"No, nothing very definite."

"Well, I myself speak from hearsay; but what I do happen to have heard, I have no objection to tell you. And then, too, it may especially befit one who is about to take up his residence yonder, to consider what that abode will be and to exercise his imagination concerning it; for what better thing could we do in the time between this and sunset?"

"Why then, Socrates, do they say it is not allowable for a man to kill himself? For, to answer the question you asked just now, I have heard Philolaus, when he was staying with us, and others also affirm that this ought not to be done; but I never heard anything very satisfactory upon these questions from any one."

62 "Well, you must keep up your courage," he said, "for it may be that you will soon hear something. You will think it strange, perhaps, that this rule alone should be unchanging, so that we cannot reason here as in other matters, and say that sometimes and for certain people it is better to die than to live. And as to those for whom it is better to die, it may seem strange that it is an impious act for these

men to confer this happiness upon themselves, and that they must needs await some other benefactor."

"Aye, Zeus be witness," said Cebes with a quiet laugh, and speaking in his own dialect.

"And indeed," said Socrates, "it may seem unreasonable, but there is perhaps some reason in it for all that. Now what is said in the mysteries in regard to these matters, that we men are under a kind of guardianship, and that we therefore ought not to break loose from it or run away, is, to my thinking, rather profound and not easy to be understood; and yet, Cebes, as much as this we may well accept—that they are Gods who have care of us, and that we men are part of the possessions of the Gods. Does not this seem to you true?"

"It does," said Cebes.

"And if your slave, one of your possessions, were to make way with himself when you had not signified that you wished him to die, should you not be angry, and punish him, if you could find any means of doing so?"

"Certainly."

"Perhaps, then, in the same way it is not unreasonable to say that a man ought not to put himself to death until God shall have sent some necessity upon him like the present one."

"Well," said Cebes, "this does seem reasonable; but then what you said about philosophers being so ready and willing to die appears like an absurdity, Socrates, if indeed what we have just said is true, — that it is God who takes care of us, and that we are part of his possessions. That the wisest men should not be more grieved than any others at leaving this service, in which the Gods, who are the best of all masters, have charge of them, is unreasonable; for no one can think that he will be able to take better care of himself for being released from this service. A foolish man, to be sure, might think that he ought to escape from any master, without reflecting that if his master is a good one he should, instead of attempting escape, cleave to him with all his strength; and so in his folly he might take flight; but any one of sense would surely wish to be ever near one who is better than himself. Thus, Socrates, the very opposite of what you said just now seems reasonable; for it behooves the wise to grieve when about to die, the unwise to rejoice."

Socrates, on hearing this, seemed to be pleased with the earnestness of Cebes, and, looking
63 round at us, said:—

"Cebes is always on the track of some argument or other, and is not at all inclined to be at once convinced by what one may say."

"Well indeed, Socrates," said Simmias, "it does seem to me too that there is something in what Cebes says. Why should men who are really wise wish to escape from masters better than themselves, and be so ready to leave them?

And it seems to me it is at you that Cebes is aiming his argument, because you are so ready to leave us as well as the Gods, good rulers though you yourself confess they are."

"You speak truly," said he, "and I think you mean that I ought to defend myself against this charge just as if I were in court."

"By all means," said Simmias.

"Come then, let me try to defend myself before you more successfully than I did before my judges. If I did not believe, O Simmias and Cebes, that first of all I were going to be with other wise and good Gods, and then also with departed men more excellent than living ones, I should be wrong in not grieving at death. But, believe me, I do hope to find myself among good men, although on this I would not so strongly insist; but that I shall go to be with Gods, exceeding good masters, this, be assured, I would affirm as confidently as anything of the kind. And this is why I do not grieve as might be expected, but am of good hope that there is something in store for us after death; something, as has been said of old, far better for the good than for the wicked."

"But, Socrates," said Simmias, "do you intend to go away keeping this belief to yourself, or will you not rather impart it to us? For it is a good which I think we ought to have in common, and if you persuade us that what you say is true, it will serve, at the same time, as your defence."

"I will try," said he. "But first we will ask Crito here what it is that he seems to have been wishing to say for some time."

"Only this, Socrates," said Crito, "that the man who is to give you the poison keeps asking me to bid you talk as little as possible, for he says that people get over-heated by talking, and that if anything of this kind is allowed to interfere with the poison, it is necessary sometimes for them to take two or three doses."

"Never mind him," said Socrates; "only let him be ready, for his part, to give two doses, or even three, if need be."

"I knew you would say so," said Crito; "but he has been pestering me a long while."

"Don't mind him," he said; "and now to you, my judges, I want to declare my reason for thinking that a man who has really given up his life to the pursuit of philosophy should take
64 courage when about to die, and be of good hope that, after leaving this life, he will attain to the greatest good yonder. And how this may be, Simmias and Cebes, I will try to tell you.

"It is apt to escape the notice of others, that they who are rightly following philosophy are devoting themselves solely to the study of dying and death. Now, if this be true, and they have been their whole life long eagerly anticipating this one thing alone, it would surely be absurd for them to be distressed when that to which they had been looking forward with the devotion of a lifetime had at length arrived."

On this, Simmias laughed.

"By Zeus, Socrates," said he, "you have made me laugh, although I am not just now at all in a laughing mood. For I am thinking that most people, on hearing what you say, would consider that you had spoken precisely the truth in regard to philosophers; at least I can answer for our Thebans, who fully agree that philosophers do in reality long for death; and they are perfectly aware too of the fact that philosophers deserve to suffer it."

"And they would be speaking the truth, Simmias, except as to their being perfectly aware of the fact. For they are not aware in what way those who are truly philosophers long for death, and in what way they deserve death, and what kind of death.

"But we will now leave these people, and talk for ourselves alone. Do we believe that there is such a thing as death?"

"Yes, of course," replied he.

"And what is it but the separation of the soul from the body? For is not dying to have the soul and the body released one from the other, so that each exists by itself? Is death anything else than this?"

"No," he answered, "this is what it is."

65 66 Most men, it is true, Socrates goes on to say, have no other aim than to obtain bodily pleasures, and hold that to live without these is no better than to

die. But the aim of the true philosopher is to attain unto truth; this, however, the body has no power to apprehend, for the senses, the instruments of the body, blind the eye of the mind, and lead us astray. Hence, philosophers cannot but regard the body as a hindrance, a disturbing element, from which the soul must be disengaged before it can arrive at perfect knowledge.

"In fact, it is quite plain that if we are ever to know anything clearly we must be released from the body, that the soul by itself may see things by themselves as they really are. And then only, methinks, shall we have that which we desire, and of which we call ourselves lovers, namely, wisdom,—after we are dead, as the argument goes to show, but not while we are yet alive. For, if while we are with the body we cannot know anything clearly, then one of two things follows; either there is no possibility of acquiring knowledge anywhere, or it is possible only after death: for then only, and not before,
67 will the soul be apart from the body, and alone with itself. And while we are yet in life, we shall be, I think, so much nearer to knowledge, the more we refrain from such contact or fellowship with the body as is not absolutely necessary, and avoid being contaminated by its nature, keeping ourselves pure from it until God himself shall set us free. And thus purified and released from the folly of the body, we shall,

as is most probable, dwell in the company of those like unto ourselves, and shall recognize of ourselves all that is genuine and pure; and this I take it, is truth. For that anything impure should lay hold of what is pure is surely contrary to divine law. Such truths as these, I think, Simmias, all true lovers of learning ought to impart one to another and to believe. Do you not think so?"

"Most assuredly, Socrates."

"Then is there great hope," said Socrates, "if this be true, that when I shall have reached that place whither I am now journeying, I shall there, if anywhere at all, gain possession of that which we have pursued so diligently in our past life. So that the journey now appointed for me is fraught with good hope to me and to every man who believes that his mind has been, as it were, purified in preparation therefor."

"Without doubt," said Simmias.

"And is not purification the very thing of which we spoke before,—the separating, as far as possible, the soul from the body, and the accustoming it to gather itself together out of every quarter, apart from the body, and to reunite itself, and to dwell, so far as it is able, both now and hereafter, by itself, freed from the bonds of the body?"

"Certainly."

"And is not the release and separation of

the soul from the body that which is called death?"

"Undoubtedly," said he.

"And true philosophers, as we have said, and they alone, are ever most eagerly desirous to release it; and this release and separation of the soul from the body is the very thing they are studying, is it not?"

"So it appears."

"Then, as I said in the beginning, would it not be absurd, if a man who had throughout his life been preparing himself to live as nearly as possible in a state of death were yet, when death came, to be distressed by it? Would not this be absurd?"

"How could it be otherwise?"

"So then, in reality, Simmias, true philosophers do make a study of dying, and death is to them, of all men, least fearful. Now consider it in the light of what follows. If they who are in every way at enmity with the body, and wish to have the soul alone by itself, were to be frightened and distressed when this had come about,—if they did not right joyfully go to
68 that place where, upon arriving, they have hope of meeting the wisdom which they have loved through life, and of being released from that body with which they were at enmity,—would not this be very inconsistent? Many a man has been willing, when some human being, perhaps a favourite or a wife or a son, has died, to

go down to the unseen world, led thither by the hope of seeing those for whom his heart yearned, and of being with them. And shall any one who really loves wisdom, and who feels strongly this same hope, that there in the unseen world and nowhere else will he meet with her in any true sense, shall he, I say, repine at dying, and will he not rather go thither rejoicing? We may be sure that he will, my friend, if he be in reality a philosopher; for then must he firmly believe that nowhere else can he find wisdom in her purity. Now if this be true, as I was just now saying, would it not be a great absurdity for such a man to fear death?"

"It would, indeed, by Zeus," said he.

"And if you see a man distressed because he is about to die, is not this a sufficient proof that he was after all not a lover of wisdom, but rather what might be called a lover of the body, and perhaps also a lover of riches and of honours, either one or both?"

"It certainly is as you say," he answered.

Only a philosopher, indeed, Socrates goes on to say, can be rightly said to possess courage, temperance, or any other virtue, and what in all others looks like these virtues is in reality their very opposite. Men submit to death because they are afraid of yet greater evils which resistance to it would bring upon them, and thus, however paradoxical the statement may appear, it is in reality through cowardice that they are courageous. In the same way they are temperate only because they know that intemperance would deprive them of certain pleasures which they value more highly than those obtained through intemperance ; so that they may be said to gain the mastery over some pleasures by reason of their subjection to others. It is like an exchange, in which one pleasure is offered for another pleasure, one fear for another fear, as if they were so many coins of different values. But the one true coin, for which alone it is right to exchange all things, is wisdom.

This exchange then, or, in other words, the deliverance of the soul from the dominion of the body, is, at the same time, a release from unworthy desires and tendencies, for it is in itself a process of purification, the result of which is courage, temperance, and wisdom itself.

"We may well believe, therefore, that they who instituted the mysteries were not mere triflers, but that there was in truth a hidden meaning in that old figure wherein they said that he who went uninitiated and unconsecrated to the world below should wallow in mire, but that he who had been purified by initiation should dwell with the Gods. 'For,' say those who direct the mysteries, 'many are the wand-bearers, but few are the true Bacchanals.' Now these last, in my opinion, are none others than they who have truly loved wisdom. Their companionship, in my life-time, I have spared no pains to gain, but have striven for it in every way. Whether I have striven rightly and succeeded, we shall, if God so will, know clearly when we have arrived yonder; and this, methinks, will be but a short time hence.

"Thus, O Simmias and Cebes, have I made my defence, to show you how meet it is that I should not grieve nor be distressed at leaving you and my masters here below, because I believe that there no less than here shall I find good masters and friends, although the mass of people are incredulous as to this. Still if I have been more successful in defending myself before you than I was before the Athenian judges, it is well."

When Socrates had thus spoken, Cebes took up the discourse and said:—

"As to everything else, Socrates, I think you have spoken truly; but in regard to the soul
70 men are very incredulous, for they fear that after it has left the body it may no longer exist, but may on the very day of death be destroyed and perish; nay, that on departing from the body it may go forth like breath or smoke, and, flying away, be dispersed abroad and exist no longer anywhere. And yet, if it could be gathered into itself and be released from those evils which you have just named, and still possess existence, then there would be great and good hope, Socrates, that what you say is true; but it would take not a little argument and persuasion to show that, when a man is dead, his soul

still exists and retains any of its faculties and its power of thought."

"You speak truly, Cebes," said Socrates, "but what shall we do? Is it your wish that we talk over these speculations together, and decide whether this be so or not?"

"I should be very glad indeed," said Cebes "to hear what opinion you hold about them."

"I really do not think," said Socrates, "that any one who heard me under the present circumstances, even if he were a comic poet, would say that I was talking idly and discoursing about things that did not concern me. So if you wish it, we will proceed to examine the subject.

"Let us consider then in some such way as this whether the souls of men after death do exist in Hades or not. There is an old doctrine, I remember, which affirms that they pass hence to the world below, and then come back here and are born into life again from the dead. Now, if it be true that after death our souls are born again into life, must they not have spent the interval in the other world? For they could not be born again if they were no longer in existence, so that, if we were quite sure that the living do come into being only from the dead, this would be a sufficient proof of the truth of what I say; but if we are not sure of this, then some other argument will be needed."

71–72 The argument which Socrates now advances is from analogy. Taking as examples life and death, waking and sleeping, he tells us that, since all things spring from their opposites or correlatives and return to them again, then, if the state of being awake generates sleep, from sleep must be derived the state of being awake; and if life generates death, from death again must come a new birth into life. Were the rule to work one-sidedly, and life to be continually engendering death, with no reversal of the process, all life would finally be destroyed; but the process of generation, instead of perpetuating a straight line from life to death, its opposite, describes a curve, which on reaching the opposite of the point it started from is bent back to this point again, and perpetually repeats the same round. The train of reasoning, of which the above is but a fragment, is thus concluded:—

"And in like manner, dear Cebes, if all things which have a part in life were to die, and after that remain in the image of death and never come back to life again, would it not follow of necessity, that finally all things would be dead and nothing be left alive? For, even if living things should continue to be generated from what remained, yet if these living things should continue to die, what could prevent all from becoming finally absorbed in death?"

"Nothing at all, Socrates, it seems to me," said Cebes; "and I think that what you say is altogether true."

"So it seems to me also, Cebes, most decidedly, and in acknowledging this we are not deceiving ourselves. There is in reality a coming to life again, and a birth of the living from the dead, and the souls of the living do exist, and it fares better for the good, but worse with the bad."

"And indeed," said Cebes, "according to
that doctrine, Socrates, which you used oft-
times to assert, that what we have learned is
nothing but recollection, — according to that, I
say, if it be true, we must have learned at some
former time what we now recollect. Now this
would be impossible unless our soul had had
73 some previous existence before coming into
this human form, so that this also would seem
to prove the soul immortal."

"But, Cebes," here broke in Simmias, "what are the proofs of this? Recall them to me, for I do not just now remember them very well."

"You will find them comprised," answered Cebes, "in one most excellent argument. When men are questioned, if the question be put properly, they give of themselves a correct answer, which they would be incapable of doing if they had not within themselves positive knowledge and right reason. Or again, if any one be shown diagrams or other things of that sort, he gives most unmistakable proof that what I say is a fact."

"If you are not convinced by this argument,

Simmias," said Socrates, "see whether examining the question in some such way as this will not lead you to agree with us. If I am not mistaken, you are incredulous on this point, how what is called learning can be recollection."

"Incredulous," said Simmias, "I am not; but what I want is to experience the very thing we are talking about, namely, recollection. By help of the explanation which Cebes has undertaken to give, I even now almost recollect and feel convinced, but none the less should I like to hear how you propose to state it."

"It will certainly be admitted," said Socrates, "that if a man recollect anything, he must at some time or other have known it."

74–76 And not only, Socrates continues, is our previous knowledge of an object recalled by the sight of it, but the image of other objects, with which in our mind it is associated, immediately recurs to us. Thus, on seeing a garment or a lute, we may be reminded of one whom we have seen use it; or, on seeing Simmias, we may be reminded of Cebes, in whose company he is so often to be found; and so in countless other instances. But when we recollect one object by means of another which is like it, we always feel that something is lacking to make the resemblance perfect, for no two visible objects, however close their resemblance, are precisely equal one to the other. We know, however, that there is an absolute equality; and of this we must have had some knowledge before we began to notice visible objects, since the very first time we beheld two objects which were called equal, we were aware that they fell short of this. Thus, it is not from external impressions that we receive our knowledge of equality, nor must the idea be confounded with objects which we call equal from their partial share in it. The idea itself is one and the same to all minds which have ever conceived it, and this immutability distinguishes it from the objects which partake of its nature; for their appearance is always changing and, moreover, never identical in the eyes of different persons.

The same reasoning is true also in the moral sphere. In a previous existence we possessed a knowledge of absolute beauty and goodness and justice and holiness; but at our birth we lost this knowledge, and can get it back only by means of that which is commonly called learning, but which is in reality recollection, and which would thus seem to be a process of recovering what time and absence had lost for us.

"We have then arrived at this conclusion, Simmias, have we not? If every pure essence whose name is forever on our lips, such as beauty and goodness, really exists, and if we find that it has been forever a part of our nature, and that we are in the habit of comparing with it and referring back to it, as to a type, all objects of the senses; if this be so, I say, must not our souls also have existed before we were born? Now if the essence did not exist before, the present argument is futile; but if it did, is there not a like necessity that our souls too existed before we were born; and that if the one did not exist, then neither did the other?"

"It does seem to me most conclusive, Socrates," said Simmias, "that there is the same necessity for both, and our argument finds a safe refuge in the equal certainty that the soul
77 and the essence of which you now speak must have existed before we were born. For nothing is so plain to me as that all of which you have spoken, beauty and goodness and the rest, do exist with the most absolute certainty. To my mind, at least, the proofs are all-sufficient."

"And how about Cebes?" said Socrates; "for Cebes also must be convinced."

"He, too, is satisfied, I believe," said Simmias, "although he is the most obstinate of men in his distrust of arguments. Still I think he is now thoroughly convinced of this, that the soul did exist before we were born. Whether, however, it will continue also to exist after our death, does not seem even to my mind to be yet settled; for that popular fear to which Cebes has just referred still stands in the way, — the fear that when a man dies his soul may be dispersed abroad, and that this may be the end of its existence. For what hinders our believing that it was generated and gathered together from some source or other and existed even before entering into a human body, and yet that when it is released from the body it may die and be destroyed?"

"You speak well, Simmias," said Cebes, "for in saying that the soul existed before we were born we seem to have proved only half, as it were, of what is necessary. If the proof is to be complete, we must demonstrate also that the soul will exist no less after death than it did before."

"This is proved already, Simmias and Cebes," said Socrates, "if you will only combine this argument with that one the truth of which we just now admitted, — that all life comes from death. For if the soul has existed before, and if, when it comes into life and receives its birth, it can be born only from a state of death, why is there not an equal necessity that it should exist after death, since it has to be born again? The very thing you demand, therefore, has been proved already. I think, however, that you and Simmias would be glad to investigate this argument more thoroughly, for I believe you fear, as children do, that when the soul goes forth from the body the wind may really blow it away and disperse it abroad, especially if one happens to die not in calm weather, but in a high wind."

And Cebes said, laughing: "Act, then, as if we were frightened, Socrates, and try to persuade us out of our fears. Or, rather, do not believe that we ourselves are frightened; but suppose there is, as it were, a child within us who has these fears. Him, then, we must try to persuade not to dread death as a bugbear."

"Then you must use," said Socrates, "day by day, some charm upon him, until you have charmed away his fears."

"But where, Socrates, shall we find a potent
78 charmer, when you have left us?"

"Greece is large, Cebes," said he, "and contains within her limits good men; and besides there are many races of foreigners, all of which you must search through for such a charmer; and you must spare neither money nor labour, for on nothing else could you lay out money more profitably. And you must make the search amongst yourselves also, for it is probable that nowhere else are you likely to find men who have more of this power."

"The search shall certainly be made," said Cebes. "But let us now, if you are willing, go back to where we left off."

To discover whether the soul is or is not of a nature likely to suffer dispersion, Socrates here examines the differences existing in the nature of things. Those which, being uncomposite or simple, have no component parts, are unchangeable and without visible form; while those which are composite, being capable of separation into their component parts, are by their very nature changeable, and, inasmuch as they are perceived by the senses, must needs be visible also. The body is included in this latter class; but to the former belongs the soul, together with every other pure essence, such as absolute beauty and equality, and all that is invisible and unchang ing and apprehended only by the mind. And as the two are unlike in nature, so also are their functions to be kept distinct one from the other. The following is an amplification of this idea.

"And did we not say long ago that when the soul uses the body as a means of perception, whether she employs sight or hearing or any other sense (for to perceive by means of the senses is to do it by means of the body), she is dragged down, by reason of the body, into things that are perpetually changing, and in trying to secure a hold of such uncertain objects as these she misses the right path, and like a drunken man becomes bewildered and falls into dizziness?"

"We certainly did say so."

"But when, independently of the body, she contemplates by her own power of vision, she hastes away to that which is pure and eternal and immortal and of a nature which never changes, and with this as being near of kin she forever dwells, whenever, that is, by isolating herself she has gained the power so to do; she rests now from her wanderings, and in this contemplation remains herself ever constant and unchanging, even as are those things which are now within her grasp."

Here follows an argument which may be thus summed up. It must be acknowledged that to rule and govern is a divine function, to be subject and to serve is a mortal one. If then we believe that nature has assigned to the soul the function of ruling, and to the body that of being in subjection, the soul is hereby proved to belong to the order of things that are divine and unchangeable. Moreover, even the body is not immediately dissolved by death, for parts of it, such as the bones and tendons, continue to exist, so far as we know, forever.

"And can we suppose that the soul, being invisible, and on her way to a place like herself invisible and noble and pure, a world worthy indeed the name of the *Unseen*, there to dwell with the good and wise God, whither, if God please, my soul also must soon go, — can we suppose, I say, that the soul, being such as she is and of such a nature, will, when released from the body, be instantly scattered to the winds and destroyed, as the mass of men assert? Far from it, my dear Cebes and Simmias; but rather is it thus: if upon her release the soul be found pure and free from all that appertains to the body, never having, willingly at least, in this life had intercourse with the body, but having shunned it and withdrawn into herself, making that indeed her constant study, — and
81 this is merely a description of a truly philosophic soul, really devoted to the study of how to die calmly, — what can we call this but a study for death?"

"That it surely is."

"When then the soul departs in this state, she goes to the world which is invisible like herself, to the world divine and immortal and full of thought; there, set free from error, folly, fears, and the fierce passions and other evils of humanity, her lot is a happy one indeed; and there, as is said also of the initiated, she abides in very truth for all time with the Gods. Do we agree to this, Cebes, or not?"

"Yes, by Zeus," said Cebes.

"But if on her release she be found unclean, and polluted by her intercourse with the body, which she has always served and loved, and by which — that is, by its passions and pleasures — she is so bewitched that she has come to believe nothing real but what has a bodily form, and so can be seen, handled, eaten, or drunk, or can serve to gratify our lusts; while, on the other hand, she has been accustomed to hate and fear and flee from that which is to the eye indeed obscure and invisible, but to philosophy perceptible and intelligible; do you think that a soul in this condition will be found pure and uncontaminated, when she is set free?"

"By no means," said he.

"Far from it; rather will she, methinks, become again entangled in that bodily form which has, by reason of companionship and intercourse and constant solicitude for the body, become an essential part of her nature. And this, my friend, we must understand, is heavy and earthy and visible; so that, when such a soul as we have described is possessed by it, she is weighed down and dragged through her fear of the invisible and of Hades back into the visible world, where, it is said, she wanders about among the tombs and graves. And indeed, in such places, certain shadowy phantom of souls have sometimes been seen, shapes such as would be assumed by souls like these, that had departed unpurified and still retaining a hold upon the visible, which indeed is the reason why they are to be seen. It is not, of course, the souls of the good, but those of the wicked, which are constrained to wander about in this way, paying the penalty of their former mode of life, which was evil; and thus do they continue to wander, until such time as they become again imprisoned in a body through the cravings of the bodily nature which accompanies them; and they are, in all probability, imprisoned in natures whose characters are like the acts to which they have devoted their lifetime."

"What kind of natures do you mean, Socrates?"

"Why, it is likely that those who have devoted themselves to gluttony and lust and drinking, and have not practised self-control, will put on the nature of asses and other like
82 animals; while those who have preferred injustice and tyranny and violence will put on

the nature of wolves and hawks and kites; and into whatever other shape any may enter, it will be one in accordance with their practice here. But is it not true that those are the happiest and the most likely to go to a better place, who have practised those civil and political virtues which go by the name of temperance and justice, but which are acquired by means of custom and habit without the help of philosophy and reason?"

"In what way are they happiest?"

"Because it is probable that they enter again into social and gentle natures, such as bees, for instance, or wasps or ants; or else that they return to the human race, and become passably good men."

"Very likely."

"But it can never be that any one who has not given his life to philosophy and departed from this world perfectly pure — any one indeed but a lover of knowledge — may enter the race of Gods. And this, friends Simmias and Cebes, is why true philosophers abstain from all the desires of the body, and stand firm, and do not give themselves up to them; not because they fear either household ruin or poverty, as do the masses and those who love riches, nor again because, like the lovers of power and of honour, they dread the discredit and disgrace of being thought wicked, and abstain on that account."

"No, indeed, Socrates," said Cebes, "for that would not befit them."

"It would not, by Zeus," he answered; "and thus those who care for their own souls and do not devote their lives to the body's interest, will bid farewell to all people like these, nor will they walk in the same paths with them, deeming that such as these know not whither they are going; but themselves believing that they ought to do nothing contrary to philosophy, and to the deliverance and purification which she works, they turn to her and follow in the way wherein she leads."

"How is this, Socrates?"

"I will tell you. They who love knowledge know that their soul, when first received by philosophy, is absolutely bound up in the body and glued fast to it, and compelled to survey the things that really exist through it as through the bars of a dungeon, and not through her own power; and that she is wallowing in all ignorance as in a mire, and is not unaware that the strength of her prison comes from her own desires, so that the prisoner is actually an accomplice in his own imprisonment.

83 "Well, as I said, lovers of knowledge know that philosophy, receiving the soul in this condition, gently encourages her and tries to effect her release, by showing that perception by means of the eyes and ears and other senses is altogether deceitful; persuading her moreover

to withdraw from the senses so far as she can dispense with them, and exhorting her to retire into herself and be self-collected, and to trust none other than herself and that part of real independent existence which she can contemplate directly by herself, but to hold as untrue whatever things, by means of different faculties, she may perceive to be varying in their different manifestations; knowing that such as these belong to the visible and to the realm of sense, but that what she sees by herself alone belongs to the invisible and to the realm of thought. Now the soul of one who truly loves wisdom believes that she ought not to resist this deliverance, but withdraws herself as much as possible from pleasures and desires and pains and fears, deeming that, when any one is powerfully affected by pleasure or fear or grief or desire, he brings upon himself no such slight evil as might be expected, like sickness or waste of property occasioned by indulging the passions; but he suffers the last and worst of all evils, and yet takes no account of it."

"And what is that evil, Socrates?"

"It is this. The soul of every man, at the time of undergoing intense joy or intense sorrow, is led to believe that whatever causes these experiences is most real and true, although in reality it is not so. And this applies especially to things visible, does it not?"

"Undoubtedly."

"And is it not in this state of feeling that the soul is most effectually imprisoned by the body?"

"How so?"

"Because every pleasure and every pain is, as it were, a nail which nails and clamps the soul to the body, and fashions her in the image of the body, causing her to believe that the judgments of the body are true. For, from agreeing with the body and rejoicing in what appertains thereto, she must perforce, I think, end by acquiring a like nature and habits; thus she will never arrive pure in the world below, but, going forth defiled by the body, will again fall into some other body and, as if sown there, take root, and thus lose her part in the communion with what is divine and pure and simple."

"You speak most truly, Socrates," said Cebes.

"And this, Cebes, is the reason why they who truly love knowledge are temperate and brave. Thus the reason given by the multitude is not the right one; or do you think it is?"

84 "Not I, forsooth."

"No, indeed; the soul of a philosopher would not reason in that way, nor would she think that philosophy ought indeed to release her, but that she might, while the very act of deliverance was going on, give herself up again to pleasures and pains, thus fettering herself anew and undertaking a hopeless and futile task; weaving, as it were, the endless web of Penelope, only with a contrary design. But she will prepare for herself a calm from these very passions, and she will follow reason, and in it forever dwell; beholding the true, the divine and the absolute, and sustained thereby. This she thinks, should be her life so long as she lives; and then, after she is dead and has reached the abode of that which is like unto herself and of her own kin, she will be free from human ills. Do not imagine, O Simmias and Cebes, that a soul which has been thus nurtured and has followed such pursuits will fear that, when released from the body, she may be dispersed and scattered abroad by the winds, and thus vanish in flight and cease to be."

When Socrates had thus spoken, there was a silence which lasted a long time, for he himself, as we could plainly see, was still absorbed in what he had been saying; and so indeed were we, for the most part. Then Cebes and Simmias began to talk a little together, and Socrates, noticing this, asked:—

"What is the matter? Does this argumen seem to you insufficient? It certainly admits of much suspicion and is open to attack, if any one should care to go into it thoroughly. If you are speaking of anything else, I have nothing to say; but if you are in difficulty about this, do not hesitate to say so, and to go over it again yourselves, if there seems to you any better way of stating it; and, moreover, to take me into your counsels, if you think I can help you to gain any clearer knowledge."

"Well, Socrates," said Simmias, "I will tell you the truth. We have both been for some time perplexed by doubt; and each has been encouraging and urging the other to speak, for we wanted to hear what you would answer, and yet, on the other hand, we shrank from troubling you with what might be unpleasant to you in this present misfortune."

Socrates, on hearing this, smiled gently, and said:—

"Dear me, Simmias, how difficult it would be to persuade other men that I do not look upon my present fate as a misfortune, when I am so little able to convince even you of it, that you are afraid I may be more unreasonable now than I have been in my past life.

"And so, it seems, I appear to you a worse prophet than are the swans, who, when they perceive that death is near, sing much more
85 fully and freely than they have sung all their life through, out of joy that they are about to go and dwell with the God whose servants they are. But men, from their own fear of death, affirm falsely of the swans that they are mourning their approaching death, and singing out of grief, not considering that no bird sings when it is hungry or cold or suffering in any

other way; not even the nightingale herself or the swallow or the hoopoe, whose songs are said to be laments. But to me it does not seem that they sing from sorrow, any more than do the swans; rather is it, I think, that being prophets of Apollo they can look into the un seen world; wherefore they sing about the good things to come, and rejoice on that day more than on any other day of their life. And I believe that I myself, a fellow-servant of the swans, am consecrated to the same God, and that I, no less than they, have received from my master the gift of prophecy; nor shall I be more reluctant than they to be set free from this life. And so you must talk and question as much as you like, so long as the Eleven permit."

"You are very good," said Simmias; "I will tell you then wherein lies my difficulty, and afterwards Cebes shall state how far he cannot accept what has been said. For I think very much as you do, Socrates, in regard to these matters; it seems to me that to know anything clearly about them in this present life is impossible, or at least very difficult; and yet not to put to the test in every possible way the common doctrine concerning them, never desisting from the task until, having searched in every direction, our strength has failed us, would be to act like complete cowards. For one of these two things must be done: we must either learr or discover how the truth stands; or, if that be impossible, we must take the best and most indisputable of human doctrines, and upon this, as upon a raft, intrust ourselves to make life's voyage; unless we can find some stouter conveyance or perhaps some divine authority to support us, and thus make the voyage more safely and securely. And so I shall not be ashamed to ask questions on the subject, now especially, since what you have just said. Thus I shall not have to blame myself in the future for not having now spoken as I really feel. The fact is, Socrates, that when I examine, either by myself or with Cebes here, what has been said, it does not seem to me that the argument has been sufficiently discussed."

"Very likely, my friend," said Socrates, "you are right; but tell me in what respect the discussion seems to you insufficient."

86–88 Simmias now proceeds to state his difficulty. The incompleteness of this argument for immortality, he says, may best be shown by applying it to harmony and a lyre, the former representing the soul, the latter the body. Harmony, a divine and invisible essence, like the soul, subsists in the lyre, which, like the body, has a form and a mortal and composite nature. Now if, as is usually held, the soul be a mixture or harmony of those elements by which the body is kept together, such as heat and cold, drought and moisture, then, when the body is relaxed and its elements are no longer properly combined, the soul, which is the result of these elements, must needs perish also. Nay, it may even be that the bodily form is the more enduring, for we know that what is left of the body does remain until it has undergone the further process of burning or decay, while from the instant of the soul's departure no vestige thereof is apparently left.

Socrates then calls upon Cebes to declare his grounds of disbelief in the argument, which he accordingly does. While he believes in the previous existence of the soul, and does not agree with Simmias that the life of the body is really the more enduring of the two, he yet fears that the soul may be outlasted by the particular body in which at the moment of death it is invested. To illustrate his meaning, he takes the case of an old weaver whom he supposes to have died while the garments woven and worn by him are still in existence. He has outlived, it is true, many sets of garments ; but death has at last overtaken him, the more durable, before time has destroyed the more perishable thing ; and so it may be with the soul ; it is constantly weaving anew, to repair the waste of the body ; but its last garment, that in which it is invested at the moment of death, is always seen to outlast the soul itself, although the weakness of its nature is shown by the decay which follows immediately upon the soul's departure. And even if we suppose that the soul comes again into being and is born and dies many times, it is yet evident that there may be limits to its powers of self-renewal, and that it may finally pass away forever. No one, therefore can know whether the death he is about to suffer may not be a final dissolution of the body.

We were all unpleasantly impressed, as we afterwards confessed one to another, on hearing them speak thus. Having been firmly convinced by the previous argument, we now seemed to be stirred up again and thrown back into doubt, not only by what had just been said, but also with a view to what might be spoken in the future; for we began to fear either that we were not capable of forming any judgment at all, or else that the matter itself was of a nature which did not admit of certainty.

Ech. By the Gods, Phaedo, I have a fellow-feeling for you. In listening to you just now, the same thing occurred to me also, and I said to myself: In what argument, then, can we trust? For the one stated by Socrates, although it seemed at first exceedingly convincing, has now fallen into discredit. The doctrine that our soul is a kind of harmony has now, as ever before, taken a wonderfully strong hold of me, and when it was stated, I was reminded that I had previously held it; but now again, as in the beginning, I stand in great need of some other argument which shall convince me that the soul of a dying man does not perish with him. Tell me, by Zeus, how Socrates pursued the subject, and whether it was manifest that he too, like yourselves, was disturbed, or whether he quietly maintained his argument; and if so, whether satisfactorily or incompletely. Relate the whole thing as accurately as you can.

Ph. Well, indeed, Echecrates, I have often
admired Socrates, but never did I admire him
89 more than on this occasion. That he should
have had an answer to give, was perhaps noth-
ing extraordinary; but what I admired most
was the gentle and gracious and approving
manner in which he listened to these young
men's reasoning, and the quickness with which
he perceived how we were affected by their
words, and the skill with which he healed our
troubles, and, rallying us even as fugitives and
men worsted in the combat, led us back again
to follow by his side and with him pursue the
argument.

Ech. And how did he do this?

Ph. I will tell you. I happened to be sitting by the side of the couch, at his right hand, on a kind of low stool, so that he was much higher than I; and he began to stroke my head and press my hair down on my neck, for it was a frequent habit of his to play with my hair.

"To-morrow, probably, Phaedo," said he, "you will have these fair locks cut off."

"So it seems, Socrates," said I.

"Not so, if you will take my advice."

"But why?" said I.

"It is to-day," he replied, "that both of us ought to cut our locks, if our argument be indeed dead and we not able to bring it back to life. And if I were you, and my own argument had escaped me, I would make an oath, like the

Argives, not to let my hair grow until I had renewed the fight and overcome the arguments of Simmias and Cebes."

"But," said I, "against two even Hercules, it is said, was not able to stand."

"Then summon me," said he, "to be your Iolaus while it is yet day."

"I summon you then," said I, "not as Hercules summoned Iolaus, but as Iolaus might have summoned Hercules."

"It makes no difference," he answered, "but one thing we must avoid."

And this is, Socrates goes on to say, the danger of becoming "misologists," or haters of arguments. For the state called μισολογία is the same in kind with misanthropy or man-hating, which is engendered from the habit of putting perfect confidence, in an uncritical, hap-hazard way, in one man after another. If any one does this, he is sure to find his confidence often betrayed, and after many experiences of the same kind, he comes to think all men knaves; but the real trouble is that he has tried to deal with men without having mastered the "science of human nature," for if he had understood this, it would have taught him that extremes of virtue and vice, as of all human qualities, are rare, and the intermediate types by far the more common. Now although this last point (that of proportion between extremes and means) does not apply to arguments, yet the former part of the illustration does, namely, a man becomes a misologist by an uncritical acceptance of one argument after another, with no scientific principle of testing arguments. Afterwards, on finding himself deceived in many cases, he comes to the absurd con clusion that *all* arguments are bad and worthless; thus cutting himself off from the means of gaining any knowledge of eternal realities.

"We must then beware of admitting into our souls the belief that there is no soundness at all in arguments. Let us rather believe that it is we ourselves who are not yet sound; but let us act like men, and bestir ourselves that we may become so,—you and the others in view of the life still before you, I in view of my com-
91 ing death. Indeed, as to myself, I fear that just now, on this very subject, I am in danger of behaving, not in a spirit of philosophy, but rather in a spirit of strife, like the uneducated. For they, whenever they are engaged in a dispute, take no thought as to the real truth of the matter in question, but are only anxious that what they say shall convince others; and I think on the present occasion I shall differ from them in this alone, that I am not anxious to have what I say convince others, unless this happen by the way, but to be myself, as far as possible, convinced. For only see, dear friend, how selfish are my considerations. If what I say is true, it is well to believe it; if, on the other hand, there is nothing at all after death, then at least, in this time that elapses before I die, I shall

not be making myself unpleasant to my friends by my laments. Besides, my ignorance will not last long; if it should, that were a misfortune indeed; but in a little while it will be done away with. Thus prepared, Simmias and Cebes, I come to the argument; and do you, if you heed my advice, take very little thought about Socrates, but much more about the truth; and, if you think I speak truly, agree with me; if not, oppose me with all your skill, taking care that I do not in my zeal deceive both myself and you, and, like a bee, depart leaving a sting behind."

92–99 Socrates now takes up the objections of Simmias and Cebes. The first is easily disposed of. To believe that the soul is a harmony of the different parts of the body is shown to be incompatible with the doctrine of its preëxistence, for it is impossible that anything can exist before the parts of which it is composed. Simmias admits that the two doctrines do not chime together, and decides at once rather to give up that of the harmony, which had merely pleased his fancy from its plausibility, than that of the soul's preëxistence, which he considers to have been already proved beyond the possibility of a doubt. After bringing forward other arguments which still further disprove the harmony theory Socrates turns to the objection advanced by Cebes. But first, as in this are involved the deepest questions of philosophy, he gives his friends an account of his own researches in this line. As a young man, he had applied himself diligently to the study of physical science, hoping, but in vain, to discover the cause of existence. Finding that these investigations threw no light on the great question "why anything comes into being, exists, or perishes," he turned to Anaxagoras, who professed to teach that mind is the cause and the controlling power of the universe. Grievous was his disappointment on discovering that, although Anaxagoras gave out indeed that mind was cause, it was practically matter which he took as his ruling principle, recognizing in point of fact no higher power than that of mere physical forces. Thus, to take the present occasion as an illustration, the fact that Socrates remains in prison would, in accordance with this principle, be ascribed solely to the action of the bones and muscles of which his body is composed. In reality, however, these very bones and muscles would have prompted and effected his escape, had he not decided in his own mind that it was juster and nobler to remain and suffer whatever penalty the Athenians might lay upon him. It is true enough that without bones and muscles he could not have carried out his resolution; but to say that they are the causes of his conduct, and that this is an example of what is called acting by mind, would be a loose kind of statement indeed. Here, as in many other instances, the cause, and the necessary attendant circumstances, without which it cannot act as cause, are confounded.

"It seems to me that the mass of men, groping about as it were in the dark, lay hold of some such attendant circumstance, and, calling it by a name which does not belong to it, pro claim it to be cause. Thus one man encompasses the earth by a vortex, and declares that it is held in place by the heavens; another imagines it to be a flat bread-trough supported by the air as by a pedestal; but the meaning of the fact that all things were originally disposed in the manner in which it is best that they should ever remain, — this they do not seek to discover, nor do they believe that it implies any superhuman power; but they think they can find some Atlas stronger and more deathless and more all-encompassing than this; while they have no faith that 'the good and binding' really binds and holds together anything at all. Now I would gladly have become a disciple of any one who could have taught me where to find such a cause as this; but since I have never been able to discover it myself or to learn of it from any one else, I will, Cebes, if you wish, point out to you the next best way, which I myself have followed, of searching for it."

"I wish it with all my heart," said he.

"I thought, after this," resumed Socrates, "that I ought to be very careful, lest, having failed to discover true existences, I should suffer what they do who gaze earnestly at the sun in an eclipse; for men sometimes have their eyes destroyed if they look at anything but its mere image reflected in water or some like substance. And just so, thought I, might my soul become altogether blinded if I looked at

things with my bodily eyes, or tried to apprehend them by means of any other of my senses. It seemed to me, therefore, that I had better take refuge in conceptions and there seek the truth of existence. Now this does not exactly correspond to my metaphor, for I do not quite concede that he who examines existence through
100 conceptions is really looking into them through the medium of images, any more than is he who examines them in the forms in which they actually appear to us. However, this is the way in which I set about it; first deciding upon the conception which I judge to be most indisputable, I then assume that what seems to agree with it is true, and that what does not is untrue."

101–107 The principle now adduced is, that there is an essential element underlying all material objects; an ideal type, which, being intangible, cannot be apprehended by the senses, although nothing but its actual indwelling gives an object true character, and a share in its own nature and attributes. Thus, to give a single example, an object is beautiful only when the type or ideal of absolute beauty, permeating it and entering into its whole nature, has left its impression upon the outward form; and every other essence or absolute idea, whatever it may be, exerts a like influence on all objects which partake of its nature. The type, moreover, of every absolute essence shuts out all that is contrary to itself. The conception of the *even* is essentially opposed to that of the *odd*, and thus cannot be admitted into any odd number. Even so the idea of death, being opposed to that of life, cannot be connected with the soul, which is inseparably associated with life; and this banishment includes also that of destructibility, which is an attribute of death.

Having by this argument convinced both Simmias and Cebes that the soul is immortal, Socrates draws from it the following inference:—

"And this, my friends, lay to heart, I beg of you. If the soul be immortal, then does she stand in need of care, not only during this period which we call life, but for all time; and we may well consider that there is terrible danger in neglecting her. If death indeed were an escape from all things, then were it a great gain to the wicked, for it would be a release from the body and from their own sin, and from the soul at the same time; but now, as the soul proves to be immortal, there is no other escape from evils to come, nor any other safety, but in her attaining to the highest virtue and wisdom. For she goes to the world below possessed of nothing but whatever training or education she may have received, and this we are told becomes either the greatest help or the greatest hindrance to the dead, at the very first instant of his journey thither. For they say that the genius of each man, to whose care he was committed when alive, has the duty of conducting him after death to that place where

all are to assemble and be judged. Thence
they proceed to the world below, each with the
guide who has been appointed to conduct him
from this world to that; and having fared ac-
cording to their due, and remained there the
necessary period, another guide, after many
and protracted revolutions of time, brings them
back here again. Now the journey to Hades
is not as Aeschylus describes it in his 'Tele-
108 phus,' for he says that 'a plain road leads to the
world below;' but it can, methinks, be neither
a plain nor a single one. Were it so, indeed, no
guide would be needed, for no one can possibly
make a mistake in following a single road; but
it seems in truth to have many partings and
turnings, as I judge from the religious rites
and the burial ceremonies in use here. The
moderate and reasonable soul follows her guide
and is not unaware of her situation; but, as I
said before, the soul which longs after the body
hovers for a long time around it and the visible
world, and is only at last, after much resist-
ance and suffering, led forcibly away by her
appointed guide. And when she has entered
into the company of the other souls, if she be
found impure or to have done impure deeds,
whether stained with wanton murders or with
other crimes akin to these, which are the works
of kindred souls, then do the other souls flee from
her and avoid her, nor will any consent to be-
come her companion or her guide. Thus must

she wander, forsaken by all, until certain periods of time have expired, when she is borne of necessity to the habitation where she belongs. But the soul which has gone through life purely and reasonably, with the Gods for her companions and guides, comes to dwell in her fitting abode."

109-114 Here follows a theory of the universe, not originated by Socrates himself, but taken from an ancient myth, in which, while not believing in its literal truth, he seems to have recognized some deeper meaning.

The earth is conceived to be a round body, perfectly balanced in the centre of the heavens, and maintaining thus its equilibrium. It embraces not only the world which we inhabit, but the pure region of upper air wherein the stars are placed. Our world is but one of the many hollows which exist in all directions round the earth, wherein are collected water, vapor, and air, — sediments of that pure ether which forms the region above. The human race known to us are described as dwelling round the Mediterranean, like ants and frogs round a pool. But just as one who had always lived at the bottom of the sea might suppose himself to be upon its surface, and imagine that the water through which he saw the sun and the stars was heaven itself, so we wrongly imagine ourselves to be on the surface of the earth, and believe that the air through which we see the stars is heaven. If we could only reach the confines of our air, we should see, were we able to bear the sight, the true heaven and the true earth, and then we should know all the regions it contains: those whose inhabitants are blessed by the continual presence of the Gods, and whose wisdom and happiness accord with this privilege, and also those terrible lower regions, where is the vast chasm called Tartarus.

"Very far away, where is the deepest abyss beneath the earth."

After sentence has been pronounced upon a soul according to deeds done in the flesh, it is conducted by its genius to the appointed place. Those who have been neither good nor bad are carried down the Acheron, a river intersecting Tartarus, to the shores of the Acherusian lake, where they remain until they are purified; the hopelessly and incurably wicked are hurled into the depths of Tartarus, whence they never come forth; but those who, while they have committed grievous crimes, are yet not past cure are thrown indeed into Tartarus, but are once a year cast forth again by the flood, and swept down to the lake, where they behold those whom they have injured in life, whose forgiveness they now implore. If this be granted, they are released; if not, they are borne back to Tartarus, and the following year again swept down to the lake; and this is repeated until they have received their pardon. But those who, purified by philosophy, are rid entirely of the body will dwell forever in habitations more beautiful than can be described. Then follows the application of the myth.

"And surely, Simmias, in view of what I have just described, it behooves us to do all whereby we may obtain in this life a share in virtue and wisdom; for the prize is a fair one, and great is our hope.

"To affirm positively that all is exactly as I have described would not befit a man of sense. But, since the soul is evidently immortal, that this or something like it is true of our souls and of their future habitations, — this, I think, it does befit him to believe, and it is worth risking his faith upon, for the risk is a glorious one indeed. And it is well that he should let such a belief act as a charm upon him, which is the reason why I have dwelt so long upon this fable. That man should be of good courage in regard to his soul, who in his lifetime has bidden farewell to all the pleasures and ornaments of the body, as foreign to and likely rather to work evil against him, and who, having striven after knowledge, and adorned his soul with no foreign ornaments, but with those which alone befit her, — moderation and justice and courage and freedom and truth, — thus awaits his jour-
115 ney to the world below, ready to set forth whenever the voice of fate shall call him. You too, Simmias and Cebes, and all the rest of you, must each one day take this journey; 'but now,' as a tragic poet would say, 'me the voice of fate is calling,' and it is well-nigh time that I should think of the bath; for it seems better for me to bathe before drinking the poison, and not give the women the trouble of washing my body."

When he had thus spoken, Crito said: "Very well, Socrates; but what charge have you to give me or our friends here, about your children or anything else, which we may most gratify you by fulfilling?"

"Only what I have always said, Crito," answered he, "nothing new; that if you will take heed to yourselves, you will, whatever you do, render me and mine and your own selves a service, even if you do not make any promises now. But if you do not take heed to yourselves, and will not try to follow in the path which I have now and heretofore pointed out, you will bring nothing to pass, no matter how many or how solemn promises you make."

"We will indeed try our best," said he; "but how do you wish us to bury you?"

"Just as you please," he answered, "if you only get hold of me, and do not let me escape you." And quietly laughing and glancing at us, he said: —

"I cannot persuade Crito, my friends, that this Socrates who is now talking with you and laying down each one of these propositions is my very self; for his mind is full of the thought that I am he whom he is to see in a little while as a corpse; and so he asks how he shall bury me. Thus, that long argument of mine, the object of which was to show that after I have drunk the poison I shall be among you no longer but shall go away to certain joys

prepared for the blessed, seems to him but idle talk, uttered only to keep up your spirits as well as my own. Do you, therefore, be my surety with Crito, though in a very different way from that in which he was surety for me before the judges. For he then pledged himself that I should remain; but you must now pledge yourselves that I shall not remain here after my death, but depart straightway. Thus will Crito bear it more easily, and, when he sees my body burned or buried, will not grieve over me as if I had suffered some dreadful thing, nor say at the funeral that it is Socrates who is laid out on the bier or carried forth to the grave or buried. For you must know, dearest Crito, that this false way of speaking not only is wrong in itself, but also does harm to the soul. Rather should you be of good courage, and say that it is my body you are burying; and this
116 you may do as you please, and in the way which you think most conformable to custom here."

Thus saying, he got up, and went into another room to bathe, and Crito followed him; but us he requested to stay behind. We remained, therefore, talking over with one another and inquiring into what had been said; ever and again coming back to the misfortune which had befallen us; for we looked upon ourselves as doomed to go through the rest of life like orphans, bereft of a father.

After he had bathed, his children were brought to him, — for he had three sons, two very young, and one who was older, — and the women of his household also arrived. And having talked with them, in the presence of Crito, and given them all his directions, he bade them depart, and himself returned to us. It was now near sunset, for he had spent a long time in the inner room. He came then and sat down with us, but he did not speak much after this. And the servant of the Eleven came and standing by him said: "I shall not have to reproach you, O Socrates, as I have others, with being enraged and cursing me when I announce to them, by order of the magistrates, that they must drink the poison; but during this time of your imprisonment I have learned to know you as the noblest and gentlest and best man of all that have ever come here, and so I am sure now that you will not be angry with me; for you know the real authors of this, and will blame them alone. And now — for you know what it is I have come to announce — farewell, and try to bear as best you may the inevitable." An. upon this, bursting into tears, he turned and went away; and Socrates, looking after him, said: —

"May it fare well with you also! We will do what you have bidden." And to us he added, "How courteous the man is! The whole time I have been here he has been constantly coming to see me, and has frequently talked to me, and shown himself to be the kindest of men; and see how feelingly he weeps for me now! But come, Crito, we must obey him. So let the poison be brought, if it is already mixed; i not, let the man mix it."

And Crito said, "But, Socrates, the sun, I think, is still upon the mountains, and has not yet gone down. Others, I know, have not taken the poison till very late, and have feasted and drunk right heartily, some even enjoying the company of their intimates, long after receiving the order. So do not hasten, for there is yet time."

But Socrates said: "It is very natural, Crito, that those of whom you speak should do this, for they think to gain thereby; but it is just as natural that I should not do so, for I do not
117 think that, by drinking the poison a little later, I should gain anything more than a laugh at my own expense, for being greedy of life and 'stingy when nothing is left.' So go and do as I desire."

At these words Crito motioned to the servant standing by, who then went out and after some time came back with the man who was to give the poison, which he brought mixed in a cup. And Socrates seeing the man said:—

"Well, my friend, I must ask you, since you have had experience in these matters, what I ought to do."

"Nothing," said he, "but walk about after drinking until you feel a heaviness in your legs, and then, if you lie down, the poison will take effect of itself."

With this, he handed the cup to Socrates, who took it right cheerfully, O Echecrates, without tremour, or change of colour or countenance, and, looking at the man from under his brows with that intent gaze peculiar to himself, said, "What say you to pouring a libation from this cup to one of the Gods? Is it allowed or not?"

"We prepare, Socrates," answered he, "only just so much as we think is the right quantity to drink."

"I understand," said he; "but prayer to the Gods is surely allowed, and must be made, that it may fare well with me on my journey yonder. For this then I pray, and so be it!"

Thus speaking, he put the cup to his lips, and right easily and blithely drank it off. Now most of us had until then been able to keep back our tears; but when we saw him drinking, and then that he had finished the draught, we could do so no longer. In spite of myself my tears burst forth in floods, so that I covered my face and wept aloud, not for him assuredly, but for my own fate in being deprived of such a friend. Now Crito, even before I gave way, had not been able to restrain his tears, and so had moved away. But Apollodorus all along had not ceased to weep; and now, when he burst into loud sobs, there was not one of those present who was not overcome by his tears and distress except Socrates himself. But he asked, "What are you doing, you strange people? My chief reason for sending away the women was that we might be spared such discordance as this; for I have heard that a man ought to die in solemn stillness. So pray be composed, and restrain yourselves!"

On hearing this, we were ashamed, and forced back our tears. And he walked about until he said that he began to feel a heaviness in his legs, and then he lay down on his back, as he had been told to do. Thereupon, the man who had given the poison, taking hold of him, examined from time to time his feet and legs, and then, pressing one foot hard, asked if he felt it, to which he answered, No; and after that again his legs, and then still higher, show-
118 ing us the while that he was getting cold and stiff. Then Socrates himself did the same, and said that by the time the poison had reached his heart he should be gone. And now he was cold nearly up to his middle, when, uncovering his face, for he had covered it up, he said, — and these were his last words, — "Crito, we owe a cock to Aesculapius. Pay the debt, and do not neglect it."

"It shall be done, Socrates," said he. "But think if you have nothing else to say."

There was no answer to this question; but after a moment Socrates stirred, and when the man uncovered him, we saw that his face was set. Crito, on seeing this, closed his mouth and eyes. Such was the end, O Echecrates, of our friend, a man whom we may well call, of all men known to us of our day, the best, and besides the wisest and the most just.

NOTES.

NOTES ON THE APOLOGY.

PAGE 5. — "*Unless some one among them happens to be a comic poet.*" An allusion to Aristophanes.

Page 7. — "*Socrates is guilty,*" etc. The first charge, that of searching into the things of heaven and those under the earth, applied properly to the Physicists, or pre-Socratic philosophers; the latter, that of making the bad appear good, to many of the so-called Sophists, or contemporary philosophers. It thus appears that Socrates was made to bear the odium attached to two rival schools of teaching, both of which he equally condemned.

Page 7. — "*In the comedy of Aristophanes.*" The Clouds was represented twenty-four years before this trial took place. There is no ground for the conjecture that it was written by order of Anytus and other enemies of Socrates with the express object of exciting popular displeasure against him. Its chief object seems to have been to uphold the old standard of Athenian education against the new philosophic school, with which Socrates was generally, though wrongfully, identified. In this comedy, we are introduced into the manufactory of ideas, or "thinking shop," where we behold Socrates sitting in a basket, which is suspended in mid-air, that he may the better examine "things in the heavens." When first brought out, the comedy was a failure, and it was only when exhibited a few years later in a revised form, that it found favour with the public.

Page 7. — "*I have nothing to do with these matters.*" Socrates always confined his attention to *anthropeia*, namely, those subjects which have a direct bearing upon human conduct, refusing to busy himself with speculations about either physical or supernatural matters, both of which he classed as *daimonia*, and held to be beyond the province of human thought.

Page 7. — "*That I undertake to teach men and charge fees for my instruction.*" Unlike most professional teachers of the day, who even when, like Protagoras, they left the actual amount of the fee to the pupil's generosity, yet expected remuneration, Socrates refused to accept anything from his followers, on the ground that he was but a fellow-learner with themselves. Moreover, "those who accepted pay for their discourses he called enslavers of themselves, because they were under the necessity of discoursing with any one from whom they received the pay." (Xen. Mem. i. 2, 6.)

Page 8. — "*Gorgias of Leontini, Prodicus of Ceos, and Hippias of Elis.*" One of the dialogues of Plato bears the name of Gorgias, the most famous of these three. He was rather the founder of a school of oratory and declamation, than a philosopher properly so-called. "At the head of the embassy (from Leontini to Athens in 427 B. C.) was the rhetorician Gorgias, who far excelled all the men of his age in oratorical power. He first invented the arts of rhetoric, and so surpassed all others in his profession that he received a fee of one hundred minas (eighteen hundred silver dollars) from each of his pupils. He astounded the quick-witted and speech-loving Athenians (in his speech to them about an alliance) by the foreign fashion of his language, for he was the first (in Athens) to use the finer figures of speech." (Diod. Sic. xii. 53.)

Prodicus of Ceos was so celebrated as a grammarian that "wiser than Prodicus" became a proverbial expression. His admirable allegory of Vice and Virtue presenting themselves for the choice of Hercules has been preserved by Xenophon. (Mem. ii. 2.)

Hippias, besides his skill in the arts and his reputation for general learning, was also a successful man in public life, having been employed by the Eleans on several missions of importance.

Page 8. — "*A man who has spent more money on Sophists than have all others put together.*" The Protagoras, 314, contains a lively description of a visit paid by Socrates to a number of philosophers quartered upon Callias, whose house was, in consequence of his hospitality, so overcrowded that he had, we are told, been obliged to convert the room used by his father as a store-room into a guest-chamber. His devotion to the Sophists led him to expend his whole fortune in acts of liberality towards them, and he is said to have ended his life in extreme poverty.

Page 8. — "*Evenus, O Socrates, ... and he charges five minas.*" The claim to universal knowledge was no unusual one among the teachers of the day. We find Protagoras, one of the most prominent of their number, setting forth his pretensions by thus encouraging a youth who thinks of becoming his disciple: "On the very first day," he says, "that you become my pupil, you will return home a better man, and the second day it will be the same again, and each succeeding day you will improve more and more." (Plat. Protag. 318.)

As we know that Protagoras not uncommonly received a fee of one hundred minas, a sum equivalent to eighteen hundred silver dollars, the charge of five minas on the part of Evenus may well have been considered moderate, especially when contrasted with the grandeur of his pretensions. We shall find this same Evenus mentioned in the Phaedo as a poet.

Page 10.—"*I shall summon the God of Delphi.*" The oracle of Apollo at Delphi, which was supposed to have been established under the immediate supervision of the God himself, was consulted by the Greeks not only for political purposes, but also to obtain opinions upon the characters of individuals, and in their eyes was invested with a peculiar sacredness. If we bear this in view, we can hardly be surprised that at this juncture, as we are told by Xenophon, the audience gave vent to loud and repeated expressions of displeasure.

Page 10.—"*He shared in the recent exile.*" When, after the capture of Athens by Sparta, in 404 B.C., the rule of the Thirty Tyrants began, many Athenians fled to Thebes and Megara, whence they afterwards returned under the leadership of Thrasybulus. This is the "exile" here alluded to. Chaerephon, called in the Birds of Aristophanes "the bat," from the blackness of his eyebrows, was satirized by some of the comic poets on account of his enthusiastic admiration of Socrates, and in Charmides is spoken of as a "kind of madman."

Page 11.—"*I cannot suppose that he is speaking falsely; that is not in the law of his nature.*" "God is not a man, that He should lie." (Num. xxiii. 19.)

Page 12.—"*By the Dog, Athenians.*" "The Dog," perhaps, stands for the dog-headed Anubis, an Egyptian divinity, identified by the Greeks with Hermes; this oath, however, is asserted by others to have been brought into use, with similar ones of an equally meaningless character, by Rhadamanthus, in order to avoid taking the names of the Gods in vain.

Page 12.—"*I went through some real labours.*" It is evident that Socrates is here alluding to the labours of Hercules.

Page 13.—"*A certain natural gift and inspiration.*" In the Ion the theory of the inspiration of poets is thus developed: "The poet is a light and winged and sacred thing, and can do nothing until he is inspired and beside himself and his mind is no longer within his con trol. . . . . God, therefore, taking away the minds of poets, uses them as his servants, even as he does the soothsayers and holy prophets; that we who hear them may know that it is not they in whom is no mind, who speak these words of priceless worth, but that God himself is the speaker, and through them is communicating with us, and that poets are only interpreters of the Gods." (Plat. Ion, 534.) And in the Phaedrus we are told: "He who without the inspiring frenzy of the Muses comes to the gates of Poetry, thinking that by art he may become a poet, fails of his end; for the poetry of him who is of sound mind is as naught in comparison with that of the man inspired by frenzy." (Plat. Phaedr. 245.)

Page 13.—"*This error obscured the knowledge that he possessed.*" "Professing themselves wise, they became as fools." (Rom. i. 22.)

Page 14.—"*It is the God who is really wise, and he means in this oracle to say that human wisdom is worth little or nothing.*" "The wisdom of this world is foolishness with God." (1 Cor. iii. 19.)

Page 14.—"*I am in very great poverty by reason of this my service to the God.*" Socrates elsewhere says that all his possessions do not exceed five minas (ninety dollars). Eupolis, a comic poet of the day, says of him: "I hate Socrates, that prating beggar, who pays great attention, forsooth, to all these other things, but as to how withal he shall be fed, to this he gives no heed at all."

Page 15.—"*They themselves often imitate me and undertake to examine others.*" This process and its results are thus described in the Republic: "The young, when they first acquire a taste for argument, regard it as a plaything, and are always using it for disputation, and in imitation of those by whom they themselves have been refuted, they try to refute others, delighting, like puppies, in tearing and rending in pieces (by argument) anybody who comes near them But, after they have refuted many, and have been in turn refuted by others, they suddenly and violently lapse into disbelief of all that they formerly held, and thus cause not only themselves, but all that has to do with philosophy, to be regarded with suspicion by other men." (Plat. Rep. 539.)

Page 15.—"*Meletus and Anytus and Lycon have attacked me.*" Of this trio of accusers, Anytus was the most influential, and at that time high in popular favor, from his having taken part with Thrasybulus in the expulsion of the Thirty Tyrants As he had during their rule suf fered great loss of property, he was probably the more desirous that his son should pursue his own trade of leather-selling, and the hatred which he bore to the whole race of philosophers was doubly bitter against Socrates, because he had influenced the young man to study philosophy. In the Meno, Anytus, incensed by a slight which Socrates, as he fancies, has cast upon statesmen, as contrasted with philosophers, utters this threat: "It seems to me, O Socrates, that you are very ready to speak evil of men. I should recommend you, if you care for my advice, to look out; probably in any city it is easier to do a harm than a good to men, and especially here is this the case, as I believe you yourself are aware." (Plat. Meno, 94.)

The two other accusers were probably influenced only by class prejudices. Meletus, who conducted the prosecution, was a young tragic poet of no high standing, in regard to whose personal appearance we are told in the Euthyphro that he had "straight hair, a not very well-kept beard, and a hooked nose." Of Lycon our only certain knowledge is that he was a rhetor, but he is probably the same who in the Wasps of Aristophanes is held up as a drunken brawler.

Page 18.—"*By Here.*" The Greek name for Juno. This oath, said to have been permitted to women, was frequently used by Socrates.

Page 18.—"*Those who sit in the public assembly.*" This was the public assembly of all the citizens of Athens, called ecclesia, which met regularly about forty times a year.

Page 21.—"*These doctrines belong to Anaxagoras of Clazomenae.*" This philosopher, born in Ionia about 500 B. C., was an intimate friend of Pericles. His scientific theories were in advance of his age, and it was probably his attempt to account for eclipses on natural principles which led to the charge of impiety preferred against him. On the strength of this accusation he was condemned to death, but the sentence was afterwards commuted to exile. His assertion that the sun was a burning mass of iron or stone, and the moon a world like our own, was regarded with horror by all sharers in the common belief which deified the sun and moon. Socrates held that such speculations as these belonged to that supernatural realm which was inaccessible to human understanding, and preferred rather to acquiesce in generally received opinions than to embrace a startling and unproved theory, like this one of Anaxagoras.

Page 21.—"*They can hear them at the theatre.*" It has been conjectured that this refers to the works of Anaxagoras, which were perhaps for sale at the theatre; but it is more probable that since the plays of Euripides, a former pupil of Anaxagoras, embody many of this philosopher's ideas, Socrates is alluding to these, when he says that these doctrines can be heard at the theatre for a drachma, which, according to some authorities, was the highest price for admission.

Page 23. — "*Now if I believe in things relating to divine beings, it surely follows that I believe in divine beings.*" Socrates seems to have in mind the doctrine of intermediary beings or agencies, thus spoken of by Hesiod: —

> "But now that fate this race has covered up,
> Men call them holy spirits upon earth;
> Beneficent, averters of our ills,
> Guardians of mortal men."
>
> (Works and Days, 121.)

The men of the golden age were supposed to have passed into a spiritual state, and to have become the guardians of living men, or rather, perhaps, an intermediary agency through which the wishes and commands of the Gods were conveyed to men.

Page 25. — "*For thy own fate,*" *said she*, "*awaits thee straightway after Hector.*"

> "And Thetis answered weeping, 'O my son,
> Soon must thou die; thou sayest true, that fate
> Hangs over thee as soon as Hector dies.'
> Again the swift Achilles, sighing, spoke:
> 'Then quickly let me die, since fate denies
> That I should aid my friend against the foes
> That slew him.'"
>
> (Iliad, xviii. 120. Bryant's translation.)

Page 26. — "*At Potidaea, Amphipolis, and Delium.*" Potidaea, a Corinthian colony, had in 432 B.C. rebelled against the supremacy of the Athenians, and this expedition was made to reduce it to subjection, which object was finally accomplished. In the Peloponnesian war, at the battle of Delium, 424 B.C., where the Athenians were defeated, Xenophon, according to one account, owed his life to Socrates.

Page 27. — "*I shall obey the God rather than you.*" "We ought to obey God rather than men." (Acts v. 29.)

Page 28. — "*Are you not ashamed to be taking thought for your possessions that they may become as great as possible.*" "For a man's life consisteth not in the abundance of the things which he possesseth." (Luke xii. 15.)

Page 32. — "*He who would be safe must lead a private life not a public one.*" "They who belong to the small class who have tasted how sweet and blessed is the possession of philosophy, know well the madness of the multitude, and that no one, so to speak, acts sanely about the affairs of the state, and that there is no ally through whose aid any one who is eager to defend the right could hope to get off in safety. Even as a man who had fallen among wild beasts, and was neither willing to follow in their evil ways nor yet capable single-handed of making front against so many fierce natures, such an one would perish before he had done any good to the state or to his own friends, and thus be of no use to himself or to any one else." (Plat. Rep. 496.)

Page 32. — "*In the style so often heard in courts of law.*" It was customary, in trials, for the defendant to bring forward all his past services to the state, with a view to exciting sympathy, and Socrates here apologizes for resorting to so uninteresting and hackneyed a mode of procedure.

Page 32. — "*I have never held any office in the state.*" When once asked how he, who never had anything to do with affairs of state, could expect to form good statesmen, he answered: "And in which of these two ways am I most occupying myself with state affairs; by engaging in them myself, or by making it my study to render as many others as possible capable of engaging in them?" (Xen. Mem. i. 6, 15.)

Page 32. — "*I was once in the senate.*" The senate was composed of five hundred members, chosen by lot, fifty from each of the ten tribes. Their principal business was to prepare the resolutions to be laid before the general assembly of the people; but they also had charge of the ordinary public revenues and exercised other important functions. The senators of each tribe had in turn the direction of affairs for a tenth of the year, during which time they were called Prytanes, and were maintained at public expense. One from among these was daily chosen by lot to preside over both the senate and the assembly, which duty Socrates, as president for the day, was on this occasion fulfilling. His refusal, therefore, to put to the vote the proposition that the generals should be tried collectively, brought the proceedings to a dead lock, until a new president could be chosen. For the legal questions involved in this celebrated trial, see Grote's History of Greece, chap. lxiv.

Page 33. — "*Sent for me to the Rotunda.*" A round, vaulted apartment, used by the Prytanes as an office; where also they dined, that they might never be found absent from their post.

Page 33. — "*Had not the government of the Thirty soon afterward been broken up.*" The tyranny of the Thirty lasted about a year only.

Page 34. — "*Those whom my accusers call my disciples*" Socrates is probably here alluding to Critias and Alcibiades, for whose misdemeanors he was sometimes held responsible, because they had in early years frequented his society.

Page 37. — "*Not of wood nor of stone was I born, but of man.*" From the Odyssey, xix. 201: —

> "Now, I pray, declare
> Thy lineage, for thou surely art not sprung
> From the old fabulous oak, nor from a rock."
> (Bryant's translation.)

Page 38. — "*Has sworn to judge according to the laws.*" The dikasts promised on oath to vote according to the laws, where laws existed; where they did not, according to the best of their judgment.

Page 39. — "*If only thirty of the votes had been changed.*" The whole number of votes was probably 501. According to Diogenes Laërtius, the whole number of the majority was 281, leaving 220 in the minority. If this statement be correct, Socrates, in speaking of *thirty* votes, was simply using a round number, without having made a close calculation.

Page 40. — "*He would have failed to receive a fifth part of the votes.*" Socrates means that Meletus, without the aid of Anytus and Lycon, would have failed to secure this number of votes, and would have been compelled by law not only to pay a fine, but to forfeit his right to institute any public process in the future.

Page 40. — "*And what counter-penalty shall I propose to you?*" In all lawsuits in which the penalty was not fixed by statute, one was proposed by the accuser, and, in case of conviction, another by the person accused; the court by custom, if not by law, being bound to choose between the two.

Page 41. — "*Maintenance in the Prytaneum.*" Citizens of high public merit, as well as victors in the games, were often rewarded by a seat at the public table in the Prytaneum. Of course this reward was ironically suggested by Socrates, as was also the penalty of thirty minas which he subsequently proposed.

Page 41. — "*That capital trials should occupy not one day only, but several.*" No process in any of the popular courts of Athens was allowed to last over one day.

Page 42. — "*A slave to the magistrates who may happen to be in authority.*" The commissioners whose duty it was to inspect the prisons and carry out the sentences of the courts were designated as the "Eleven," from their number, each of the ten tribes furnishing one member chosen by lot, the eleventh being a scribe.

Page 44. — "*It is not much time that you will gain.*" Socrates means to say that, as he was seventy years of age, his enemies, in the natural course of events, would not have had long to wait for his death.

Page 45. — "*I did not think I ought to do anything unmanly.*" "Socrates," Xenophon tells us, "although he could easily have procured his release had he been willing to do any of the things contrary to law which are wont to be done in court, preferred rather to die, abiding by the laws, than transgressing them to live." (Xen. Mem. iv. 4, 4.)

Page 45. — "*That moment when men are most gifted with prophetic power.*" The ancients believed that dying men had the gift of prophecy. Patroclus, when dying, foretells Hector's death, as Hector does that of Achilles.

Page 47. — "*In calling you judges, I name you indeed rightly.*" Socrates reserves this form of address — *my judges* — for those who voted in favor of his acquittal, while he addresses the whole body of dikasts as citizens or Athenians.

Page 48. — "*The great King himself.*" The King of Persia.

Page 48. — "*Those true judges.*" In the Gorgias we find this legend, relating to judgment after death. Pluto, it is said, complained to Zeus that the souls of the dead went astray, and did not get to their appointed places. On investigation, the reason was discovered to be this: judgment being given on the day of death, indeed, but while men were yet in the flesh, their souls, no less than those of their judges, were still clothed in a material body, which, together with the garments they yet wore, interposed, as it were, a double veil and thus rendered clear vision impossible. To obviate this difficulty, Zeus appointed his three sons — Aeacus, Minos, and Rhadamanthus — as judges in the world below, and ordained that only after death, when divested of body and raiment, should souls receive their sentence; that thus they might appear before the tribunal of Hades in all the nakedness of their guilt.

Page 50. — "*Thinking themselves to be something, when they are worth nothing at all.*" "For if a man think himself to be something when he is nothing, he deceiveth himself." (Gal. vi. 3.)

NOTES ON CRITO.

PAGE 54. — "*Has the ship come from Delos, on whose arrival I am to die?*" See the opening of Phaedo for an account of this ship.

Page 55. — "*So say they who order these things, you know.*" An allusion, as in the Apology, page 42, to the commission of eleven who had charge of the prisons.

Page 55. — "*Thou shalt reach the coast of fertile Phthia.*" From the Iliad, i. 363. This quotation is slightly altered from the original, where Achilles speaks in the first person.

Page 65. — "*Is it right . . . . to render evil for evil?*" "Recompense no man evil for evil." (Rom. xii. 17.) "See that none render evil to any man." (1 Thess. v. 15.)

Page 67. — "*Any one, above all an orator.*" It was customary, at Athens, whenever a law was about to be repealed, to appoint proper orators or advocates to plead its cause as that of a defendant.

Page 68. — "*To instruct you in music and gymnastics.*" As gymnastics included the whole training of the body, so did music that of the mind, — comprehending not only poetry and music in the modern sense of the word, but literature and philosophy as well.

Page 71. — "*Not even to be a spectator at the games.*" As is well known, the games were made a subject of national pride and glory, and the success of the victor reflected as much honour upon his country as if he had won for it some splendid victory in war; the most eminent poets of the day were called in requisition to celebrate his triumph, and his statue was erected by his grateful fellow-citizens in the sacred race-ground. Such being their character, the games were naturally attended by all the leading men of Greece; and thus the absence of Socrates was the more conspicuous. The Isthmian games here alluded to were celebrated at the Isthmus of Corinth, in honour of Neptune.

Page 72. — "*But you preferred neither Lacedaemon nor Crete.*" Socrates frequently spoke in terms of great admiration of the constitutions and laws of these states, and of the obedience yielded to them by the people.

Page 73. — "*Say Thebes or Megara, which are both well governed.*" These cities would have been naturally chosen by Socrates as a place of residence, as they were moderate oligarchies, and sympathized politically with Sparta, for whose government Socrates professed so great an admiration.

Page 76. — "*Even as the Corybantes imagine they hear the sound of the flutes.*" The Corybantes were priests of the Phrygian Cybele. The worship of this Goddess, like that of Bacchus, was celebrated by furious dances, and by music of so boisterous and exciting a character that the bare recollection of its peculiar strains had power to put the mystic into a sort of transport, which rendered him oblivious to all outside sights and sounds.

NOTES ON PHAEDO.

PAGE 78.—"*List of speakers.*"—Echecrates of Phlius is supposed to have been a Pythagorean philosopher.

Phaedo, the narrator of this dialogue, was a native of Elis, and of noble birth. At an early age he was taken prisoner of war, and sold as a slave in the market at Athens, but was redeemed, it is said, either by Socrates himself or by one of his friends. He was now, for the first time since his capture, about to return to his native city and had probably stopped at Phlius on his way. Of his subsequent career we only know that he founded the Elean School of Philosophy.

Apollodorus is mentioned in the Apology as one of the four friends who offered to be security for the fine proposed by Socrates. His excitable nature is exhibited in the latter part of this dialogue. So ardent and passionate was his devotion to Socrates, and so vehemently was he in the habit of expressing it, that, like Chaerephon, who also is mentioned in the Apology, he had gained for himself the title of "the maniac." In another of Plato's dialogues he says: "I make it my daily care to know what Socrates says and does." Xenophon relates that after the trial he complained that it was the injustice of the sentence which most distressed him; whereupon Socrates, 'smiling and stroking the head of Apollodorus, answered: 'But dearest Apollodorus, should you prefer to see me put to death justly rather than unjustly?'" (Xen. Apology, 30.)

Simmias and Cebes were the authors of several philosophical dialogues, and in the Phaedrus, 242, Socrates speaks of the former as having an inordinate love of argument.

Crito, although many years older than Socrates, seems to have been his most devoted friend; his loving services, which began by rescuing him from the drudgery of the work-shop, ending only with the performance of the last offices of friendship.

Page 80. — "*The ship in which Theseus once embarked for Crete.*" The famous expedition of Theseus to Crete, where, by the help of Ariadne, he killed the Minotaur, thus releasing Athens from her yearly tribute of seven youths and seven maidens who were sacrificed to the monster. Plutarch tells us that, by the constant renewing of her timbers, the semblance at least of the original ship was preserved, and she was actually used for the embassy here mentioned.

Page 82. — "*And from Megara, Euclides.*" Euclides was the founder of the Megarian branch of the Socratic philosophy, in which branch dialectics formed the most prominent part.

Page 82. — "*And how about Aristippus and Cleombrotus?*" A reproach is perhaps here intended for these two disciples, who had not taken the short journey from Aegina to be with Socrates in his dying hour. It is said that Cleombrotus, after reading the Phaedo, threw himself into the sea in a fit of self-reproach.

Page 83. — "*And Xanthippe, whom you know.*" Socrates married Xanthippe at the age of fifty. Although her name has become a byword for a shrew, she is not wanting in defenders, who urge in extenuation of her faults of temper the peculiar trials to which she was abjected by her husband's indifference to the temporal welfare of his family.

An episode mentioned by Xenophon (Mem. 2, 2) gives us a far from disagreeable impression of her character. Her son, Lampsacus, it appears, has been provoked into answering her improperly, and Socrates takes this occasion to remind the youth of the debt of gratitude he owes her, and by the enumeration of her many acts of self-sacrifice and devotion places her before us in the light of a tender, though perhaps over-anxious mother. Here, too, she is represented as an affectionate, impulsive woman, in contrast with whose heartfelt laments the cold words of Socrates make him appear in so unpleasant a light that we have need to be reminded, in mitigation of his apparent heartlessness, that he was but carrying out the ordinary Greek idea of conjugal and family relations.

Page 85. — "*Cultivate the Muses.*" The literal translation is, "Practise the art of music." As poetry and literature were included under the head of music, this injunction to Socrates did not imply anything further than that he was to put words into a metrical form. The opening of the hymn to Apollo, here mentioned, is quoted doubtfully by Diogenes Laërtius, and runs thus: —

"Hail, Apollo, King of Delos;
Hail, Diana, Leto's child!"

Page 87. — "*In your discourses with Philolaus.*" Philolaus was a philosopher of the school of Pythagoras, who, like his master, taught that everything should be referred to mathematical principles.

Page 87. — "*What better thing could we do in the time between this and sunset.*" By Athenian law, no executions were allowed to take place in the day-time.

Page 88. — "*What is said in the mysteries.*" This is not an allusion to the Eleusinian mysteries, but in all probability to the mystic system of Pythagoras, this saying being presumably one of his esoteric precepts, which were classed among the "ineffable secrets." Regarding these, the strictest silence was enjoined, and the key to their meaning was possessed only by the disciples of Pythagoras and those initiated by them. They seem to have been symbolic legends, purporting to explain the origin of the universe and the various phenomena of nature, from their previous acquaintance with which the initiated hoped to escape all hardships in the future life, and be admitted straightway into the presence of God.

Page 92. — "*At least I can answer for our Thebans.*" The Thebans, the fellow-citizens of Cebes, and indeed all the other inhabitants of Boeotia, were noted at Athens for their heaviness and want of intellect.

Page 95. — "*So then, in reality philosophers do make a study of dying.*" "I die daily." (1 Cor. xv. 31.)

Page 95. — "*Many a man has been willing to go down to the unseen world.*" The allusion is probably to Alcestis and to Orpheus, who braved the terrors of Hades for the sake of those they loved.

Page 97. — "*Many are the wand-bearers, but few are the true Bacchanals.*" To be allowed to join the Bacchanalian processions, it was only necessary to carry a wand composed of the narthex, a plant with a pithy stalk, the same in which Prometheus is said to have conveyed the fire from heaven. The large number of these merely formal participators in the rites, when compared to the few truly inspired worshippers, gave rise to this proverb, which was afterwards used to illustrate the frequent compliance with outward observances in contrast to the rarity of real performance of duty. We can hardly hear it without calling to mind the solemn words: "For many be called, but few chosen." (Matt. xx. 16.)

Page 99. — "*Even if he were a comic poet.*" Socrates here refers to Aristophanes, who, in the comedy of the Clouds, represents him, to use the words of the Apology, as "babbling about things concerning which I know absolutely nothing at all."

Page 99 — "*There is an old doctrine, I remember, which says.*' Olympiodorus thus comments upon this passage: "The Orphic and Pythagorean doctrine is that souls enter again into a body, and then again go forth from it, and thus perform many times a circle." It would appear that in almost all pre-christian faiths, belief in immortality involved belief in the soul's preëxistence. On page 105 Socrates further explains why to his mind the two doctrines are indissolubly connected.

Page 101. — "*We must have learned at some former time what we now recollect.*"

> "Our birth is but a sleep and a forgetting;
> The soul that rises with us, our life's star,
> Hath had elsewhere its setting,
> And cometh from afar.
> Not in entire forgetfulness,
> And not in utter nakedness,
> But trailing clouds of glory, do we come
> From God, who is our home."
>
> (Wordsworth's Intimations of Immortality.)

Page 101. — "*Or again, if any one be shown diagrams.*" In the Meno, another dialogue of Plato, we have an exhibition of this experiment, a slave-boy, on being questioned by Socrates on the relation of certain geometrical figures, giving correct answers "out of his own head."

Page 106. — "*You must use . . . . some charm upon him.*" It was probably to the charming and healing influence of "good words," that Socrates is here alluding, as in Charmides, 157, where he says that they "act as charms in the healing of the soul."

Page 108. — "*Can the soul, being invisible and on her way . . . to dwell with the good and wise God.*" "And the spirit shall return unto God who gave it." (Eccl. xii. 7.)

Page 108. — "*Worthy indeed the name of the Unseen.*" The literal meaning of the word Hades is *unseen*, although in Cratylus, Socrates asserts that it is derived from *eidenai, to know*, namely, all things good and beautiful.

Page 109. — "*Rather will she become again entangled in that bodily form.*" This passage is almost reproduced in Milton's Comus, 467: —

> "The soul grows clotted by contagion,
> Imbodies, and imbrutes, till she quite lose
> The divine property of her first being.
> Such are those thick and gloomy shadows damp
> Oft seen in charnel vaults and sepulchres,

Lingering, and sitting by a new-made grave,
As loath to leave the body that it loved,
And linked itself by carnal sensuality
To a degenerate and degraded state."

Page 110.—"*Will put on the nature of asses and other like animals.*" The theory of metempsychosis was that the souls of men and animals alike were detached fragments from an universal soul-life which pervaded the whole universe, so that there was no essential difference between the souls of man and beast.

Page 112.—"*Compelled to survey the things that really exist as through the bars of a dungeon.*" "For now we see through a glass darkly." (1 Cor. xiii. 12.)

Page 115.—"*The endless web of Penelope, only with a contrary design.*" The object of Penelope's task being to undo what had just been accomplished, that of the soul to do over again what philosophy had just done away with.

Page 116.—"*The God whose servants they are.*" The swan, the symbol of music, was sacred to Apollo, both from its supposed gift of song, and from the power ascribed to it, in common with the raven and the crow, of looking into the future.

Page 121.—"*To-morrow, probably, you will have these fair locks cut off.*" Cutting the hair was a customary sign of mourning.

Page 121.—"*I would make an oath, like the Argives.*" The Argives, on being defeated by the Spartans, took an oath not to cut their hair until this disgrace had been retrieved.

Page 122.—"*Against two, even Hercules, it is said, was not able to stand.*" A proverb arising from the legend spoken of by Socrates in Euthydemus, 297, as follows: "I am much inferior to Hercules; and even he was not able to fight at the same time both the Hydra (who, being a she-Sophist, could, if one head of the argument were cut off, shoot forth many fresh ones in its place), and also another enemy in the shape of a crab (likewise a Sophist), who had, I believe, just put into port after a sea voyage. But he (Hercules), when this new monster began to assail him, called upon Iolaus, who, coming to the rescue, gave him efficient help."

Page 124.—"*Like a bee depart, leaving a sting behind.*" An allusion, perhaps, to these lines on Pericles, by Eupolis, the comic writer. "Thus he bewitched men; and thus, alone of orators, did he leave behind him the sting of his pointed words."

Page 126.—"*One man encompasses the earth by a vortex.*" A

theory of Empedocles. In Greek astronomy the sky was regarded as a solid vault, in which the stars were fixed.

Page 126. — "*Some Atlas stronger than this.*" They hoped to discover some heretofore unknown physical force which might account for all phenomena, both physical and spiritual.

Page 128. — "*There is terrible danger in neglecting her*" (the soul). "For what is a man profited, if he shall gain the whole world and lose his own soul." (Matt. xvi. 26.)

Page 129. — "*Aeschylus in his Telephus.*" A lost tragedy of Aeschylus. The line here referred to has not been preserved in its original form.

Page 129. — "*The religious rites and the burial ceremonies in use here.*" It was customary to perform funeral rites every month, in honour of Hecate and the other infernal deities, for which ceremonies a spot where three roads crossed was generally chosen.

Page 131. — "*Very far away, where is the deepest abyss beneath the earth.*"

> "Rayless Tartarus
> Deep, deep in the great gulf below the earth."
> (Iliad, xviii. 14. Bryant's translation.)

Page 131. — "*Habitations more beautiful than can be described.*" "Eye hath not seen, nor ear heard, neither have entered into the heart of man, the things which God hath prepared for them that love Him." (1 Cor. ii. 9.)

Page 134. — "*He then pledged himself that I should remain.*" In the Apology we learn that Crito was one of the four who offered to stand security for the payment of his fine.

Page 136. — "*Stingy, when nothing is left.*" This refers to a proverb, found in Hesiod's Works and Days, 367, which Seneca thus translates: "Sera parsimonia in fundo est," "*'Tis a sorry thrift at the bottom of the cup.*"

Page 138. — "*A man ought to die in solemn stillness.*" A Pythagorean saying.

Page 138. — "*We owe a cock to Aesculapius.*" Aesculapius, the founder of the art of healing, was struck dead by Zeus, because he persisted in restoring men to life. Many scholars, especially Grote (Plato, ii., p. 195), take these words in a literal sense, thinking that they betoken, on the part of Socrates, an anxious desire to fulfil his religious duties after the accustomed fashion of his country. Others see in this dying request the legacy left by him to his friends of his unshaken conviction that through death a life of health is opening before him.